THE CEO

CHIEF ENERGIZING OFFICER

OF YOU

YOUR OWN UNIQUENESS

Marsha Petrie Sue, MBA

Discover the Emotional Reality of Success

Communicating Results Press
Scottsdale, Arizona

The CEO of YOU; Discover the Emotional Reality of Success
By Marsha Petrie Sue

Copyright© 2002 by Marsha Petrie Sue

Printed and published in the United States of America
By Communicating Results Press
PO Box 15218, Scottsdale, AZ 85267

Third Edition: January 2005

ISBN 0-9703807-4-7
Library of Congress Control Number: 2002095471
$17.95

Dedication

With deep love, affection and heart connection, I dedicate
this book to my husband, Al, the smartest, most logical and
centered person I know.

This book is about taking control and accepting
responsibility. I hope the words inspire you to look at
all the opportunities available and the talents you have
for success in your own life.

Acknowledgments

I acknowledge Bill Webb for helping me with
the first edition of this book, Rosalie Hydock for
her "English teacher" eyes, Norma Strange for giving
the CEO a new look, and Nancy Greystone for her
common sense approach. Thanks to all my peers,
clients, friends and family that made the first
edition such a huge success.

What can
be
added
to the
happiness
of a man
who is
in
health,
out of
debt,
and has a
clear
conscience?
❖ *Adam Smith*

Contents

✦

The CEO of YOU

Before
everything else,
getting ready
is the
secret
of **success.**

◆ *Henry Ford*

Introduction

My speaking career began with a public seminar company presenting workshops to thousands of people around the world. During the breaks, people would approach me with questions and comments. In retrospect, I don't think people knew what they wanted to ask.

"My boss (client, group) would never let me try that." Have you already tried it? Did you lose a job or client by using the tool? How do you know it won't work?

"I want things to be better." Better than what? Better how and for whom? By when? What's your plan?

"I want my life to be more in control." Control of what? Why? If you were in control, then what? Do you control anything now?

"I want people to respect me." What does respect mean to you? Why is respect important to you? What will it give you that you don't have now?

Keep an open mind as you read this book. Think about what will work vs. what won't work. Successful people never stop learning and challenging themselves. I guarantee this book will give you tools to move to the next level.

The key is to take action. Many people think reading a book or attending a seminar will anoint them with success. The outcome is dependent on the steps you put in gear after reading the book. Learn to take risk, try new approaches and continue to move forward in a positive fashion. My personal experience has taught me that focus, discipline and passion are absolutely necessary for continued success. And each of those elements are controlled – or not controlled – by us as individuals.

No excuses. You are the CEO of YOU.

THE
CEO

HR

+ Selectively choose who is on your team

+ Select personal life services carefully

+ Hire the best people

PR

+ Establish a good first impression

+ At the end of every day, think of the five great events of the day

+ Get proper rest and exercise and start eating more healthily

+ Stay away from gossip

SALES

+ Develop an elevator speech

+ Sell YOU in 30 seconds or less

+ Stay caught up

+ Focus on what you have

CONTINGENCY PLANNING

+ Eliminate "what if" thinking

+ Visualize your next position

+ Encourage bootstrap thinking

+ Encourage flexibility

R&D

+ Address the future

+ Invest 2 percent of your gross annual income in YOU

+ Do you know the goals of your company?

+ Be a lifelong learner

FINANCE

+ Lead a simpler life

+ Pay cash

+ Limit charge cards

+ Save money, even when you think you can't

IT

+ Hire a computer tutor

+ Embrace technology

OF
YOU

Chapter 1

❖

You are the company

You are *it*.

You are the company, the organization, the main source of everything.

Because you are this entity, you also need an organizational chart. Therefore, you must create success categories that help you focus on each area of your professional and personal life.

The chart opposite offers you a picture of the structure of your company. Use it to help you focus on what is working well and what you might change to make your company more productive and profitable.

If you think this is a weird way to take charge of your life, answer these questions:

+ **Who is responsible for your learning?**
+ **Who is responsible for your own development and the research to get you where you want to be?**
+ **Who should decide what you want out of life?**
+ **Who should determine what people say about you after you are gone?**
+ **Who should be able to tell others what your talents are and what job you want to strive toward next?**
+ **Who should determine the value of you as a human resource?**
+ **Who should sell your talents and capabilities to others?**
+ **Who is responsible for the promotion of you – your public relations?**
+ **Who should help you embrace the application of technology?**
+ **Who should inform you about what you need to learn?**
+ **Who should be responsible for putting food on your table or a roof over your head?**

Nothing is lost upon a person who is bent upon growth; nothing is wasted on one who is always preparing for his work and life by keeping eyes, mind, and heart open to nature, men, books, experience. Such a man finds ministries to his education on all sides; everything cooperates with his passion for growth.

⋄ *H. Mabie*

The answer to each question is: YOU!

As CEO – the Chief Energizing Officer – you must take responsibility for overseeing each of these departments. This does not mean you do them all yourself, but that you do enlist the services of professionals to guide you.

Let's look at each department and the need, benefit and expected outcomes.

R & D (Research & Development) department

Every company needs growth. Growth and future success are typically created in the R & D department. R & D means research on what is working and what needs to be developed. The CEO must be aware of what is being done to prepare for the future. This includes continually improving and polishing tools that were not needed in the past but will be needed in the future because of expected growth.

Brian Tracy taught me many years ago that I must invest 2 percent of my gross annual income in me. I now spend about 10 percent or more! Take a moment now to determine what you should be spending:

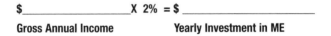

$\underline{\hspace{2cm}}$ X 2% = $ \underline{\hspace{3cm}}$

Gross Annual Income   **Yearly Investment in ME**

Are you investing this amount in your future, every year?

The term "Learning Organization" is very popular today, and has been fostered by Peter Senge in his landmark studies of successful organizations (*The Fifth Discipline*). You achieve good employment and a successful life by learning about all aspects of your environment. Can you answer the following questions?

Aim at the
sun
and you may not
reach it;
but your arrow
will
fly
far
higher
than if
aimed at an
object
on a level
with
yourself.
❖ J. Hawkes

Do you know the goals of your organization and associates?
If not, ask what they are.

Does your team have an understanding of the vision of your superiors, all the way up to the top level?

Your superiors often just have to be asked.

Do you have the tools needed to succeed in the job of your dreams?

If not, what are you doing about it?

Many people, from Peter Drucker to Bill Gates, believe that success lies in our interpersonal skills – the ability to manage confrontation, deal with difficult people, enjoy successful communications, and stay motivated and positive. These are learned skills. You are not born with them. You are expected to develop and use them confidently and skillfully.

I am always intrigued when people say, "Well if my company won't pay for it, I'm not going to do it!" Putting your success and future in the hands of others will not always get you where you want (and deserve) to be.

Many people who attend my talks invest in themselves. They buy books, tapes, seminars, and take classes for their own improvement. They have decided to take charge of their future and their success. Have you?

What next step can you take toward your success?

Turn your car into a university on wheels. Many studies show the value of learning in your car or when exercising. Listening to music is fine, and a good way to decompress. But it is also chewing gum for the brain. Wouldn't you much rather turn the useless time in your car into learning time? Just a quick five-minute run to the store can ignite new thinking by listening to an expert to affirm a strategy or solve a difficult problem.

Everybody wants to be somebody; nobody wants to grow.

✦ *Goethe*

Time. You decide how you use your time. Use it to build and grow yourself. Use it for the research and development you deserve.

I have trained myself to use time more effectively. The operative word here is *trained*. One of the biggest barriers to achieving success and taking control of your life is the use of the spare time you have. This is the only resource we all share equally. Do you use your time to increase your knowledge?

I have a need to better use my time more effectively for research and development. Training myself to have the guts, energy, and time, to return to school for my graduate degree was not easy. The outcome for me is the life I am now living. I know I would not be living the life of my dreams if I had not completed my graduate degree. This is not necessary for everyone – it was for me.

And the training continues. The benefit of constantly listening to tapes in my car gives me the outcomes I continue to strive for. Sharing tapes with friends, investing in new learning resources, taking every opportunity I can in research and development is not a need – it is a must.

Contingency planning department

Contingency planning in companies is the strategy that allows for change. It's also called *"what if"* thinking. *What if* plan A doesn't work? Then you have plan B ready to roll.

When contingency planning is perceived as a tool, the outcome will be positive. You are setting the stage to be flexible and ready for change. So what if the next position you have your eye on is axed? Do you wilt and fold? Become a victim of circumstance? Or do you choose to pull yourself up by the bootstraps and say, "OK, what is the next

Make
big
plans,
but
change
your
plans as
time
changes.
✦ *Marchant*

opportunity, challenge, want, wish or hope I have for my future?" You have a choice here.

And there's the rub. "What if" thinking can be debilitating. Here is a real-life story: A woman attending one of my classes two years ago was visibly upset. I had shared the story of how I met my husband, Al, by hiring a matchmaker, mentioning that I then became a wife, grandmother and mother all on the same day.

She approached me during the break and said, "Oh, I can't take the risk of using a dating service, because what if I meet someone who is not truthful about his background, and what if we fall in love and get married? What if there are some medical issues about his background that he doesn't tell me! What if we have a child and the baby is born with some medical issues, or maybe is retarded? What if my new husband can't deal with the medical problems and leaves me? What if I am supposed to raise a child with disabilities by myself? What will I do? What if the child has really bad medical problems and I can't find care for them?"

I wanted to yell, "STOP!"

A kind observer stopped her instead, saying: "You are going to 'what if' yourself into a nervous breakdown and you haven't even called a matchmaker yet!"

The perfect response.

Pay attention to the conversation you are having in your own head. Contingency planning and what if thinking should lead you to alternative ways to succeed – just in case the current plan doesn't happen.

Outlook, attitude and approach have everything to do with successful contingency planning.

Plans
get you
into
things but
you
got to
work
your way
out.
⟡ *Will Rogers*

Flexibility is key here:

+ **Are you flexible enough to allow yourself to fail?**
+ **To be resilient in situations that have unfavorable results?**
+ **To move past broken plans?**
+ **To pull yourself up, dust yourself off and move on?**
+ **To chalk up disaster to life, learn from it, and start again?**
+ **To understand that failure brings you an easier path to success?**
+ **To know that every event has a learning nugget planted in it?**
+ **To see the horse poop and know there has to be a pony somewhere?**

Easier said than done! But doable.

When I moved from California to Atlanta, it was a big risk. I had commuted for two years and was then asked by Westinghouse Financial to pick up my life and relocate to the city in which I was working. This seemed reasonable and obviously was a good choice for the company.

But wait! I had to leave my friends, family, security – everything I had known for more than 40 years. I needed a contingency plan. What if the project I was working on failed? What if I was stranded in Atlanta with no job? I consulted my dear friend, who is an attorney. He had given me sterling advice in the past.

"How about asking for an employment contract?" he asked.

Oh, hadn't thought about that! So the deal was struck that if the project did not work out, I would receive a full year's salary and they would pay for my move back to California.

Do you have a need for stability? I do! What are the contingency plans you have set up so your confidence soars and the what ifs don't get in your way?

Human resources department

Who are the people you hire and team up with to be in your corner, to be the leaders to help you run your company?

Our grand
business is not to
see what lies
dimly
in the distance,
but to do
what
lies
clearly
at hand.
⋄ *Carlyle*

Do you selectively choose who will be on your team, or do you take a willy-nilly approach? Do you interview each member to ensure they will fit into your success scheme? These people should all be considered part of your team and should be selected carefully:

- Your doctor – keeps you at your best health
- Your attorney – makes sure you are operating above board
- Your dentist – keeps your pearly whites shining
- Your accountant – manages your taxes properly
- Your financial planner – keeps your portfolio properly balanced
- Your banker – for loans, cash and high credit rating
- Your stockbroker – keeps your risk factors in mind and helps your money grow
- Your grocery clerk – specials, favors and deliveries in the time of need
- Your butcher – to impress at the right time during that important dinner party
- Your dry cleaner – clean and pressed on a moment's notice
- Your minister – counselor, connection to the larger world and spiritual balance
- Your family – critical support, not just at critical moments
- Your partner – even more critical support
- Your friends – even when things are not going so well
- Your computer tutor – keeps you in the groove with technology
- Your politicians – speak your piece to an ear that hears
- Your beautician/stylist/barber – so you can get that trim on a moment's notice
- Your clothing store salesperson – keeps you informed of special sales and when that outfit comes in with your name on it
- Your cobbler – people DO notice your heels!
- And anyone else who adds to the success of YOU.

You can't
do
everything
yourself.
Hire
the
best
to fill the
gaps
or
your
life
will
fall
through the
gap.
⋄ *Marshall Petrie*

Invite supportive people to be on your team. Hire people who are the best at what they do, not just cheap. You are a worthy growing company, and you deserve to have the best of the best on your team. Seek out their advice and their expertise.

You do not have to be the guru and keeper of all knowledge. You do not need to know everything.

I learned this many years ago from my father, who was an accountant. His clients expected expertise on every decision – to manage their taxes, secure a plan for the future, to protect their hard-earned money from being eaten up by taxes. My dad worked with financial planners and stockbrokers and would refer the right professional to solve the exact issue. He belonged to the Lions Club, the Elks, the Masons, the March of Dimes. He networked to bring the best human resources to himself and his clients.

Do you have your human resource plan? Have you enlisted the best of the best for your company? I know very little about investment, but I know Al, my husband, has enlisted some of the best to oversee the placement of our money.

If you go to a professional to have a service rendered and you do not receive a satisfactory outcome, product or service, do you put them on notice? I know of many people who don't, because they "don't want to hurt their feelings."

I say, pooh on their feelings!

I want to be the CEO and be in charge, which means I set the expectations. No service? Goodbye. The competition is too keen to have my human resource department keep poor performers. Does a successful company keep poor performers? No. If it does, it won't be successful for very long. Expect the best and that's what you will get.

Our chief want in life is somebody who will make us do what we can.

✦ *Ralph Waldo Emerson*

We sometimes must make decisions quickly – especially in the human resources arena. When you hear voices saying, "Oh, do it" or "Oh, no, don't," listen very carefully. Typically, our internal voice is that gut feeling, taking all the experiences we have had and sending us a subliminal message. So listen to the subliminal message. Listen to the first message, because your negative self talk can sabotage your intuition.

I had a need to have a professional edit this book. My first round of finding an editor was unsuccessful – though I did spend some major bucks ferreting out the wrong editor. The first person I tried was sweet, recommended by a peer, but I had no idea what my needs were. And my gut was yelling at me – "Great person; wrong for your need!"

So after three or four months of not much happening, I had to bite the bullet and tell this editor that I was taking a different focus on the book. Luckily, one of my peers in the National Speakers Association – Bill Webb – rescued me. He is the consummate professional, knows the editing bit and has tremendous credibility in our industry and the publishing world. As I initially met with Bill, my intuition was screaming to me, "You'd better hope he will take on your project. He is the perfect fit for the outcome you want!"

Are you willing to invite new people onto your team, both professionally and personally, who will add the talent you need to become the CEO and take control? This is where that old phrase kicks in – "You create your own luck!" And you do it through your own human resources department.

Sales department
Yep, you are in sales.

Chance opportunities make us known to others, and still more to ourselves.

✦ *Francois de La Rochefoucauld*

Step 1

Begin developing your "elevator speech." Be able to sell YOU to the boss, an executive, or someone you want to work with. Reduce it to 45 seconds or less. Here is my elevator speech, which is always under construction:

"Hi, I'm Marsha Petrie Sue. I present keynotes and workshops to associations and companies that want to improve communications, customer service and personal power of their executives and employees, ultimately improving profitability and productivity."

Here is the outline. Fill it in for yourself:

Hi, I'm_____. I work with_____ and have had tremendous success in_____. My talents range from_____ to_____. Being a lifelong learner and working in challenging environments is critical to my success. (Or something along that line.)

Memorize your elevator speech. Practice it. Say it confidently, to anyone, anytime. You must be able to pull this out of your hip pocket and say it at a moment's notice.

Step 2

Keep up on current events and your reading – popular books, magazines, and professional journals. When chatting with peers and superiors prior to the start of a meeting, talk about nuances of your industry, cutting-edge stuff, not how are the kids, the cat, the dog. Strut your stuff when you can, without being arrogant, self-centered and ego crazed. If you don't toot your own horn, no one else will.

Step 3

Take time every three months to write down all the talents you have and how you apply them. Tom Peters says in his book *Work Matters* that the typical resume is passé. You

If a man
empties
his purse
into
his
head,
no man
can
take
it away
from him. An
investment
in
knowledge
always pays
the best
interest.
✦ *Benjamin Franklin*

should market and sell your talents. Be able to tell ANYONE, with confidence, what you do well, and what your goals and aspirations are. He says all of this must be rehearsed, practiced: If you stammer through your greatness with another person, especially someone who can hire you for that perfect job, your credibility is doomed.

Focus on what you have, rather than what you don't have. Because of our frequent negative thinking, we often dwell on what we can't do or what we don't have. Focus instead on everything you know and do so well. If you don't, no one else will do these things for you.

Step 4

On a regular basis, understand your value in your marketplace. Do an Internet search on www.monster.com, hotjobs.com, or any of the other sites that can give you so much information on jobs, geography, job titles, and job descriptions. Don't like your salary or wage? *Change jobs!* If you don't have the skills or education – get them!

I knew being promoted at GTE was very competitive. My research proved to me that promotion was many times dictated by a college degree. The three cut piles were high school graduate, bachelor's and then master's degrees. I needed an MBA – so I went back to the University of Phoenix, studied until my brain was fried for 22 months and in 1985 received my master of business administration degree. Two weeks after receiving my MBA, I was promoted.

Public relations department

Three seconds. That's the time you have to influence another human being. Will you establish good or poor public relations? Three seconds.

Fields are **won** by those who **believe** in **winning**.

✦ TW Higginson

The *first* image people see determines if this will be a good interaction or a poor one, and the first characteristic that becomes apparent is attitude. Is yours positive or negative? How do you appear to others?

Whether it's you or someone else who needs an attitude tune-up, there are tools to help you rev up your engine. Here are some ideas to brighten the worst outlook and put you in the mood to be motivated and to motivate others:

+ Count your blessings daily and give thanks.
+ Think of seeing two sweet children holding hands.
+ Drive by a flower shop with beautiful flowers displayed in the window.
+ Pass a hospital and realize how lucky you are not to be in it!
+ When you lie your head down on the pillow at night, think of five great events of that day. You will have days, as we all do, that are mind-boggling tough.

I usually think of only three before I am fast asleep. By replacing negative events, you promote more restful sleep. Falling asleep with only the problems and issues of the day in your head will usually promote restlessness. Brian Tracy says, "You become what you think about."

+ Get proper rest and exercise and start eating more healthily.
+ Do not let pettiness at work, school, or in your personal life hold power over your success.

I have read that the No. 1 reason people gossip is to subconsciously make themselves feel better. As another person is dragged over the coals behind their back, the people stoking the fire don't feel too wonderful about their own situation.

Here's quite a morale booster:

Small
opportunities
are often the
beginning
of
great
enterprises.
❖ *Demosthenes*

A teacher in New York decided to honor each of her seniors in high school by telling them the difference they each made. Using a process developed by Helice Bridges of Del Mar, California, she called each student to the front of the class, one at a time. First, she told how the student made a difference to her and the class. Then she presented each of them with a blue ribbon imprinted with white letters which read, "Who I Am Makes a Difference."

Afterward, the teacher decided to do a class project to see what kind of impact such recognition would have on a community. She gave each of the students three more ribbons and instructed them to go out and spread this acknowledgment ceremony. Then they were to follow up on the results, see who honored whom and report back to the class in a week.

One of the boys in the class went to a junior executive at a nearby company and honored him for helping him with his career planning. He gave him a blue ribbon to put it on his shirt. Then he gave him two extra ribbons, and said, "We're doing a class project on recognition, and we'd like you to go out, find somebody to honor, give them a blue ribbon, then give them the extra blue ribbon so they can acknowledge a third person to keep this acknowledgment ceremony going. Then please phone me to tell me what happened."

Later that day, the junior executive went in to see his boss, who had a reputation for being a grouchy fellow. He told his boss that he deeply admired him for being a creative genius.

The boss was quite surprised. The junior executive asked him if he would accept the gift of a blue ribbon, and placed the ribbon right on his boss' jacket, above his heart. Then, before he gave him the last extra ribbon, he asked, "Would you do me a favor? Would you take this extra ribbon and

What
it lies
in our
power
to do,
it lies
in
our
power
not
to do.
✦ *Aristotle*

pass it on by honoring somebody else? The young boy who gave me these ribbons is doing a project in school. He wants to keep this recognition ceremony going and find out how it affects people."

That night, the boss came home and sat down with his 14-year-old son. He said, "The most incredible thing happened to me today. I was in my office and one of my execs came in and told me he admired me and gave me a blue ribbon for being a creative genius. Imagine! He thinks I'm a creative genius! Then he put this blue ribbon on my jacket above my heart that says 'Who I Am Makes A Difference.' He gave me an extra ribbon and asked me to find someone else to honor.

"As I was driving home today, I started thinking about whom I would honor with this ribbon and I thought about you. I want to honor you. My days are really hectic, and when I come home I don't pay a lot of attention to you. Sometimes I scream at you for not getting good enough grades in school and for your bedroom being a mess, but somehow tonight, I just wanted to sit here and, well, just let you know that you do make a difference to me. Besides your mother, you are the most important person in my life. You're a great kid and I love you!"

The startled boy began to sob uncontrollably. His whole body shook. He looked up at his father and said through his tears, "I was planning on committing suicide, Dad, because I didn't think you loved me. Now I don't need to."

This is a true story, and we need to keep it going. If you have anyone who means a lot to you, I encourage you to send them this message. You never know what kind of difference a little encouragement can make to a person. Send it to all of

In
prosperity prepare
for a
change;
in
adversity
hope
for
one.
✧ *Burgh*

the people who mean anything important to you, or send it to the one or two people who mean the most. Or just smile and know that someone thinks that you are important, or you wouldn't have received this story in the first place.

Finance department

The buck stops – and starts – here. You decide where to spend each dollar you earn. Many people have this in common: They never feel they have enough money or time to plan for the future. The fact is, though, that we have exactly enough time and money to do whatever we choose to do.

I am amazed that in the nineties – probably one of the strongest decades of economic growth most of us have ever experienced – more personal bankruptcies were reported than in the previous major economic downturn. Why? Lack of discipline and the will to apply these simple steps:

1. Lead a simpler life.

2. Pay cash.

3. Limit charge cards.

4. Save money, even when you think you can't.

1. Lead a simpler life. Do you read magazines and watch advertising that demand you change with the seasons, the trends, or the neighbors next door?

The influence of the environment is tremendous and can lead you to poor choices. Super Bowl ads cost millions of dollars a minute; magazines need to be held with both hands because of the extra pages of advertising; eye-level shelves in grocery stores are premium spaces for products – all advertisers hope to influence you. Do they? And how?

Born and raised in Southern California, I truly believed materialism was what life was all about. Our home in the

Beware of little expenses.
A small leak will sink a great ship.

✧ *Benjamin Franklin*

rolling hills of the coastal community of Palos Verdes was a beautiful Spanish-style stucco house with a pool. I lived there for my first 15 years. My parents frequently hosted parties, with the menu usually featuring filet mignon and lobster.

Our summers were spent either on the 36-foot cabin cruiser my father built in our back yard, or at the family lakeside home at Browns Lake, Wisconsin. These were the standards and role models I was raised with. I thought it was normal.

When my parents divorced, a hard reality unfolded. We had nothing. Everything was leveraged or loaned, borrowed or past due. Mom and I moved out of the beautiful family home and into a two-bedroom duplex Mom bought on a shoestring.

But the high-consumption model was set for life. After I graduated from college in 1968, my goal was to have it all. I interpreted that to mean: Spend as much as fast as you can.

Years later, I remember my dad coming to visit my home in Westminster, California. He walked into the house quite disgusted, saying, "Well, I can see you are buying American! Two German cars is disgusting and materialistic!"

That comment went right over my head!

But hard reality hit me two years later when I divorced my first husband. I had no idea what we had or – more importantly – what we didn't have. We had been living the life of Riley. Materialism....

After working myself out of another financial fiasco, I set a goal: Know where your money is and where it's going!

Al, my current husband, taught me how to lead a simpler life. We do not live in the biggest house in Scottsdale – a beautiful home, to be sure, but certainly not lavish. We don't drive the fanciest cars or go on the most lavish vacations, but you have never met two happier people.

Everything
in
the
world
may be
endured,
except
continual
prosperity.
◆ *Goethe*

2. Pay cash. This is simple. Don't buy anything unless you have the cash in your hand or know exactly where the funds are coming from. If you don't have it, don't spend it!

Want to plan for a vacation? Take $10 a week, put it in an envelope labeled "vacation" and don't plan until you have at least 75 percent of the money saved. Reduce the complexity of your financial obligations. Use automatic deposit for your paycheck or dividends. If you don't see it and touch it, you have less chance of misusing your money.

Contact the companies you receive bills from each month – insurance, utilities, mortgage and so on – and establish automatic payments. Each will mail, e-mail or fax you a form requesting the needed account information. Be patient, because this may take two months, but it's certainly worth the time spent.

With the companies that are not able to set up automatic payments, consider paying quarterly, semiannually or annually. The less you have to think about, the more in control you will be – and life will be simpler for you.

Soon technology will offer even more options, and cash may become outmoded sooner than we think. Bill Gates says that in the near future, we could all have a microchip implanted in our wrist. Need a soda at a vending machine? Wave your wrist in front of the optical scanner and the price of the drink will be deducted from your bank account automatically. This technology is already in place at many highway toll stations – such as FastTrack™. Drive by and your FastTrack account is reduced by the amount of the toll. Scary! But efficient!

3. Limit charge cards. Some of the stories you hear today are unfathomable: One woman was proud to announce her

In
character,
in manners,
in
style,
in
all
things, the
supreme
excellence
is
simplicity.
✦ *Longfellow*

ownership (or so she called it) of more than 152 credit cards – and had a balance due on all of them! Al and I have three credit cards. I use American Express™ for my business; we have a Visa™ for our personal expenditures; and Al has a company American Express™ card.

We receive "invitations" to accept more cards weekly, sometimes it seems like daily, because our credit is good. We plan to keep it that way. But aren't we all amazed at the credit limits these cards offer?

If you are a parent, have you noticed that even your children are receiving credit card applications? Tear them up immediately. Chop them into tiny little pieces! Receiving the cards is not fatal – using them is.

4. Save money. Extra cash because of a bonus? Invest it. In the long term, a diverse stock portfolio will grow your money. Consolidate your investment portfolio into just a couple of families of funds. This has taken us a few years to accomplish, but it is so much easier to track.

Teach these simple steps to anyone who will listen and learn them yourself. If you are in a financially secure position, congratulations! Those of us who are secure are in the minority.

Karen, my husband's daughter, is teaching her son, Wes, well. A teenager, Wes has a debit card. His monthly allowance is put on the card. Wes had to figure out from month to month what he can buy. The first couple of months, the money was gone early in the month. Wes learned a good lesson. Making choices in purchases and how the money was allocated was his responsibility. When shopping for the music CD he *had to have*, or the new pair of jeans he *had to have*, he learned what his real choices were.

Man
is
equally
incapable of
seeing
the
nothingness
from which
he
emerges
and
the
infinity
in which
he is
engulfed.
◆ *Blaise Pascal*

Respect for money is learned. Are you teaching people around you this lesson? Do you know it yourself? We all have a need for stuff, but we also all have a need to save. Being able to have financial stability and being monetarily secure is the responsibility of every human being. Who knows what the future will bring? Are you financially ready?

How will you meet your future needs? Do you know the difference between a SEP-IRA, Roth IRA, traditional IRA and a SIMPLE IRA? How about Keogh plans? What are the benefits of real estate investments, second trust deed investments, or even a family trust? And here is the big question – do you have a will, and if you do, when was the last time you updated it?

My prayers were answered during my first session with my financial planner years ago. I learned how much I didn't know. I had to develop an understanding of what my risk level in investments was. Then what was the investment vehicle that was best for my situation and my financial goals. I was so overwhelmed with information. But that was a very important financial turning point. Many years later, much learning and an incredible partner have moved us to financial security. How are you doing with your finances?

Marketing department

Your marketing is a level deeper than just the sales and PR departments. Marketing is how you position yourself in your life with other people – how they perceive you and interact with you. As with public relations, you never have a second chance to make a first impression. There is an interesting reason for this, and it's called the "First Brain."

Part of our thinking process is filled with all our experiences and the results of those experiences, what you can call "old

Thinking is the talking of the soul with itself.

✧ *Plato*

thinking." The First Brain acts like a gatekeeper to the rest of your brain – and that gate is either open or closed. If the gate is closed, you don't accept ideas that are new or different from your own. You are not able to take a risk because old thinking gets in the way. You are not able to change.

Example: You meet someone for the first time. You look at them and size them up. You make a decision – which takes three seconds or less – and you will like that person, or not. You scope them out and say to yourself, "I can just tell I'm going to like them. They are my kind of people."

And when you decide not to like the person? You say to yourself, "I don't think so." Your First Brain is closed. You hear little or nothing of what the person says, because your First Brain has locked the gate to the rest of your brain. Not only has your public relations failed, your marketing can't get on track.

If you are willing to open your thinking gateway (First Brain), new information and alternative ideas can flow in. You can then get a better picture of the other person, because you are more flexible. Your public relations strategy works more effectively. Your marketing is then right on target.

Example: We all need to understand that mature audiences need more time to make a decision. If you are not from that generation – and don't value its differences – you close your First Brain and become impatient with that audience needing more time to decide. That is your choice. It's not that you can't open your First Brain – it's because you choose not to.

Most savvy business people determine on a regular basis that there are three asset values when assessing their business – fixed assets, variable assets, and intellectual assets.

Intellectual assets encompass all your actual job skills, but the major impact derives from your emotional state. Daniel

You
cannot
teach
a man
anything;
you can
only
help
him to
find
it
within
himself.

✦ *Galileo*

Goleman coined the term "emotional intelligence" to help us understand the importance of interpersonal skills as an intellectual asset. Emotional intelligence traits are derived from your socialization, and are learned as you move from childhood to adulthood. When you improve your interpersonal skills, you become the CEO of YOU!

IT – technology department

Unless you are a computer wizard, hire a computer tutor. I have a couple of them – one for my database, and one for software. They help me use technology more effectively and are among my best friends.

One of the reasons I returned to school for my master's degree was to learn about computers. My knowledge of technology was nil. Slowly but surely, I am feeling more capable and competent. Bill Gates says in his book *Business at the Speed of Thought* that if by 2005 you are not using technology daily, you will be considered work-illiterate. Even if you dig ditches, supply janitorial services or are the CEO, technology is here to stay.

Those who embrace technology advancements will succeed; those who do not, will not! Very simple. This has been a hard realization for me. Is it for you, too?

I had to learn the importance of learning new applications, using technology effectively, and not allowing new applications to steal my time. I do not use a PDA (Personal Digital Assistant) yet – it is cumbersome for me and I like showing people my goals when I speak directly from my hard-copy planner.

Some people shouldn't be using a PDA. They fumble and muddle around with it – what a time waster!

I believe
the
true
road to
preeminent
success
in any
line
is to
make
yourself
master
of that
line.

＊*Andrew Carnegie*

The message here is to embrace technology, apply what is appropriate for you at that particular moment, but don't spend hours on equipment or software that will not help you.

Example: PowerPoint slide shows. PowerPoint makes me very nervous as a professional public speaker. More times than not, I have seen poor results from using PowerPoint. The screen loads improperly; slides are missing; lighting in the room is awful; or the lights have to be off so you can see the screen; people are soon asleep; the program crashes.

And on and on.

I am going to learn to use PowerPoint because I know it shows that I am on top of technology. I will simply use it as I have used overhead foils in the past – to enhance the presentation, not become the presentation!

The good news is that PowerPoint brings everyone into the new millennium. The bad news is that 75 percent of the people using it don't know how! The point? Only use technology to enhance what you are doing, not overwhelm it!

In running my speaking business, I now know technology can make or break me. Web sites are an expected marketing tool in business today. Many naysayers in the speaking industry feel this technology is not necessary to succeed. I'm sure there is a very small percentage of speakers who were well established before the Internet era who do not need a Web site. I also know what my site has done for my credibility. The links on my site to other resources allow my clients to connect electronically.

E-mail is a critical component of my business, with or without a Web site. I want to stay connected to my network, clients, family and friends, no matter where my travels take me in the world. I can do that with e-mail. The recipients can pick up messages when they want and respond at their convenience.

It is easy
to
learn
something
about
everything,

but difficult
to learn
everything,
about
anything.
✧ *Emmons*

The people in my database receive my leadership e-zine newsletter on the latest trends and issues of industry on a monthly basis in a format comfortable for them. Kept short and sweet, this is one of the best tools as a CEO I use today. Connecting, keeping myself remembered and providing valuable information can only be done with this technology. Snail mail gets tossed, phone calls are not returned and personal appointments are cancelled.

How are you using technology to make life easier and more efficient?

You are the company. Reflect upon the chart (pg. 6) and resolve now to make visible in your life the fact that you can truly become your own CEO.

Nothing is more despicable than a professional talker who uses his words as a quack uses his remedies.

✦ *Francois de la Mothe Fenelon*

Chapter 2

✦

An attitude of gratitude

Hardening of the attitude?

Attitude will make us or break us. Do you have an attitude of gratitude or a hardening of the attitude?

If you find yourself making the wrong choices, poor decisions, or failing when you truly believe success should be yours, a negative attitude may be the cause.

In a *New York Times* study, hundreds of managers and business owners were asked to identify the No. 1 characteristic they looked for in hiring and promoting employees. The majority of those polled said the most important characteristic is a positive attitude, because you can't train someone to be optimistic. They either are or not. But the polled group agreed you can train someone to learn a skill. So it is your responsibility to learn more about the skills underlying an attitude of gratitude.

Symptoms of a hardening of the attitude

People don't understand you – No matter what you say, and you know you are saying it right, people don't get it. The lights are on and no one is home. Even the stock boy at the grocery store can't understand your simplest requests, like "Where would I find aspirin?"

You are caught in a rut – Instead of going forward, you always seem to be slipping backward. You have great goals but never can do the right things to move toward achieving those goals. It's like being a hamster on a cage wheel – you

We will
always
have
time
enough, if
we
will
but
use it
aright.
✦ *Goethe*

run and run and never get anyplace, until you fall off the wheel and have to take time out because you are really sick! The light at the end of the tunnel really is an oncoming train!

Any kind of change bothers you – You know life is busy and always changing, but lately even good change makes you tense. They just upgraded all the software and you have told them how much time it will take you to learn the new system. Why can't they just let you use the old software? Don't they understand?

You are a bully – The only way people hear you and pay attention to what is important is when you get in their faces. You stand up for your rights but violate the rights of others. You feel this is the only way you can get anything done.

You are a doormat – It's easier not to say anything. People don't listen anyway, so why waste the energy? You are not comfortable standing up for your own rights and you let other people violate your rights because this way at least people like you.

No time for compliments – People should know they are good at certain things and you really shouldn't have to waste your precious time telling them. They may get a big head if reminded too often how good they are.

You are boastful – Why not tell people all the great things you've done in your life? They, of course, won't notice that you have larded up the story a bit. Anyway, it makes you interesting, which is more than most can say about themselves.

Positive people seem to drift away from you – You look around at your circle of friends: They are negative, toxic, and have tons of problems. What is wrong with these people? They whine and bemoan everything and expect you to fix it all for them. They are LOSERS!

I know
no
evil
so great
as the
abuse
of the
understanding
and yet
there is
no
one vice more
common.
✦ *Steele*

You find yourself often depressed and often full of doubt and worry – Life is really depressing. How can you smell the roses if you are pretty sure the steps you're going to take aren't the right ones? You are hesitant to accept change because it may be the wrong step or in the wrong direction. What will they say if it doesn't work out right? Where is your rose garden?

You can't sleep at night – You lie awake nights chewing on the what-ifs: the coulda-woulda-shouldas in your life. You wake up tired.

Thinking about what you don't have has become the center of your thought process – Why are other people so lucky? Why are people always winning the lottery and it's never you? Life's not fair. You feel that you deserve more than you are getting.

People don't seem responsive when you talk about important events in your life – Why do people always have to turn the topic back to themselves? If they listened to you they would be a lot better off because you have a lot of experience and they need to hear it!

Gossip keeps you connected – You can't do your job without having more information from your supervisor and everyone else in the building. Your boss doesn't seem to understand that you need this data.

So many things are wrong and broken – The world has so many problems. You get depressed and demoralized because people just don't fix them!

Why are so many people so negative? Maybe it's largely because of how you were raised. By the time you are 18, you have heard "you can't," "you'll never be able to," "don't try" more than 180,000 times. The old recordings of all the sour input come from our parents, ministers, teachers and peers.

Habits
form a
second
nature.
✦*Jean Baptiste Lamarck*

All the actions we take during the day filter through these recordings.

Do more than one of these symptoms sound familiar to you? And if you are so trapped, do you have the desire to do something about it? That's what this book is about – learning, reviewing, and applying tools that enable you to change. You can transform your negative thinking into an attitude of gratitude.

My mom and dad constantly fought about everything. Mother was a wonderful cook and Dad loved to eat. But there was always something wrong with just about every meal. Mom would cook pot roast and make slits in the top of the meat and slip cloves of garlic to flavor the meal. Wonderful! Mom knew Dad hated garlic – so she put the garlic in the roast just to spite Dad.

I didn't realize this until my adult years when I was cooking a meal for my dad and he said, "No GARLIC! A little bit of garlic is like being a little bit pregnant. You either are or aren't!" Mother had developed a very subtle way to antagonize Dad and feed the negative atmosphere.

What kind of environment are you feeding your loved ones? An attitude of gratitude or a hardening of the attitude?

The environment in our house was typically hostile and negative. My sister, eight years older than I, was a real challenge for my parents. I remember Mom putting me in the backseat of the car and driving the streets of our neighborhood at night, searching for my sister because she had once again run away from home. Eventually she would show herself because she was tired and hungry. Then, of course, they would fight.

We vacationed every summer on Catalina Island in Dad's

Man is
what
he
believes.

✦ *Anton Pavlovich Chekhov*

boat, the *Marpet*, and moored just off the Tuna Club. Most evenings the harbor master, Chick, would come by the boat after curfew and announce that my sister had been picked up for missing curfew. My parents would get dressed and go ashore to have her released from the Avalon jail. Another argument. Another fight. I thought all families went through this kind of turbulence.

What kind of role modeling is going on in your environment, both at work and at home?

What a shame! We had a beautiful home, wonderful friends, took fantastic vacations and threw incredible parties. The environment created a negative spin for me because much of my life was about materialism and not love, pessimism and not optimism. Hardening of the attitude was a disease inherited among family.

My husband, Al, introduced me to his family a few months after we met in 1992. I couldn't believe what I saw – a mom and dad who really loved each other! A brother and sister who actually talked to one another – and cared about the other. A grandson who called his grandparents every week to see how they were doing. Everyone always had an optimistic outlook, with something positive to say. This was a whole new world for me!

Al was raised in a military environment, moving cross-country every few years. Usually they camped along the way, sleeping under the car during the rain, wrapped in a plastic tarp to stay dry, and cooking meals on a campfire. What wonderful bonds his family built through the years, with no fancy vacations or expensive birthday gifts, just love and caring for themselves and each other.

When we lost Al's mom, she and Pop had been married 61 years. Their relationship took hard work because they were separated by his work in the Marine Corps and war.

The
root
of this trouble
is in the home;
and those
who talk about
more
nurseries, better
playgrounds, curfews,
better milk, and
more
dance
halls are perhaps
diminishing
the
effect
but not
removing
the cause.
✧ *Fulton Sheen*

People today do not seem to want to devote that kind of energy to their relationships. They are not looking for the positive outcomes – their disease of hardening of the attitude turns the tables, and every event revolves around themselves, not other people. Such behavior stems from the negative talk we inflict upon ourselves.

Change your environment

Have you noticed how the negative swirls around you so often? The news, for instance. Tragedy, killings, crime, wrong-doing and on and on. This is one reason I will not listen to the news in the morning. All it does is bring me down before I've even gotten up. Rather, I listen to someone who motivates me, a book on tape, or recordings I make for myself with motivating quotes.

Yes, I make my own personalized motivational tapes. I record all the bits and pieces accumulated over the years. This is one reason you will find positive quotes and statements throughout this book. I capture these snippets in my daily planner, then record about 30 to 45 minutes worth of good stuff. This also corresponds to the time it takes me to get ready in the morning. People often ask me for a copy of my tape, so I have included "Clips and Bits" on the last tape in my audio learning program, *Out of the Puddle, into the Pond.*

This positive information plays back in my head through-out the day. The fact is, you do become what you think about. A good example of why this works relates to listening to music in your car: You are driving and singing along the highways and byways. People are staring at you and you know they're saying, "Who is *that* weirdo?" You arrive at your destination and turn the engine off. The last song playing becomes your

True love's the gift which God hath given, to man alone beneath the heaven. The silver link, The silver tie, which heart to heart, and mind to mind, in body and in soul can find.

⟡ *Walter Scott*

anthem for the day and keeps popping into your head at random (and weird) times throughout your day. Have you ever caught yourself saying, "Stop it – I can't stand hearing that song one more time!"

And even when you go to sleep at night you are still humming and singing that same old last song. You say to yourself, "Boy, I sure hope it's a new song tomorrow because I am sick of this one!"

Why do people pay good money to have a bad attitude, get scared out of their wits, or feel depressed? I am not enamored by the movie industry: There are some very funny and entertaining movies out there, but by and large, they have too many killings, too much gore, and are just plain depressing. Life can be difficult enough without adding to the negative picture!

We become what we think about. Think negative thoughts – become a pessimistic person. Think positive thoughts – become an optimistic person.

The next time you start to gripe about life and all that's going wrong, remember there is always something to be thankful for:

+ **The mess to clean up after a party because it means that you've been surrounded by friends.**
+ **The taxes you pay because it means that you're employed.**
+ **The clothes that fit too snug because it means you've enough to eat.**
+ **The shadow that watches you work because it means you're in the sunshine.**
+ **The spot you find at the far end of the parking lot because you are capable of walking.**
+ **The complaining you hear about our government because it means that we have free speech.**
+ **The lady behind you in church who sings off key because it means you can hear.**

Our self-love is ever ready to revolt from our better judgment, and join the enemy within.

❖ *Steele*

- The piles of laundry and ironing because it means your loved ones are nearby.
- The lawn that needs mowing, windows that need cleaning and gutters that need fixing because it means you have a home.
- The huge heating bill because it means you are warm.
- The weariness and aching muscles at the end of the day because it means that you have been productive.
- The alarm going off early in the morning hours because it means that you are alive.

Mind your thinking

You become what you think about, so learn to replace negative self-talk with positive self-talk.

Self-talk? Do I talk to myself?

Of course you do – at 600 to 800 words per minute!

Our lives are like a movie: Each person we meet, each conversation and event – even our perceptions of these events, *especially our internal reactions to them* – are experienced within the framework of our self-talk. Our negative – or positive -- self-talk acts like a lens. It reveals every experience in a negative or positive light. How we self-talk reveals our frame of reference.

If we don't like the negative frame of reference, we can stop the movie, shift the lens over to the positive, and thereby replace the darker frame of reference with one that is more positive.

If this means changing old habits for you, we know two things for sure: It may not be easy at first, but it certainly is doable.

The technique I use is called "*StopFrame.*" When you catch yourself saying something negative to yourself, stop in midstream and say, "*StopFrame.*" Then replace that negative sentence with positive information.

Gratitude
takes
three forms:
a
feeling
in the
heart,
an
expression
in words,
and a
giving
in
return.
✦ *John Wanamaker*

Here is an example of how I have used this technique: When I turned 50, I began to experience hot flashes. You *know* all the negatives associated with menopause.

StopFrame.

I discovered, and immediately liked, the words I learned from my audiences in South Africa, Australia and New Zealand. Their term – and frame of reference for describing certain effects of menopause – is "power surge," "My own private summer," or my favorite, "I'm not having a hot flash, I'm self-basting."

Much better. New frame of reference: Well, I self-baste a lot, especially at night. (Al once told me that we need asbestos sheets; he was afraid I would burn down the house!)

And when I get up in the morning it is not a pretty sight. I've been sweating all night, my hair is glued to the side of my head and has formed a red point at the top of my skull. I look like Woody Woodpecker! I sometimes look at myself in the mirror, and say "Oh brother, look at you! What a mess! You'll never make sense of that."

StopFrame.

I replace that negative frame of reference with, "Boy! You are sure going to look and feel a lot better when you get out of the shower!"

That's a whole different kind of self-talk. And the changing of self-talk must be done continuously, not just once in a while. If you continue to replace negative thoughts with positive ideas, you change your thinking and therefore your habits.

Another example: You walk into a formal meeting; the agenda has you speaking right after the boss. You say to yourself, "They won't like what I have to say. I will probably get to

The
happiness
of your
life
depends upon
the
quality
of your
thoughts,
therefore
guard
accordingly;
and take
care that you
entertain
no
notions
unsuitable
to virtue
and
reasonable
nature.
✧ *Marcus Antoninus*

the podium and forget my name. I can't believe I volunteered for this!" The negative becomes a self-fulfilling prophecy.

If we tell ourselves we will mess up and be a failure, we will rarely let ourselves down! StopFrame the negative self-talk and say, "What a wonderful opportunity to shine and let these folks know the great job I am doing."

I have learned from the experts, who agree that this negative thinking originates inside our own heads. Think about the events in your life that have created the unique you and the way you process information. Let me share with you some highlights – or rather, lowlights – that will show you what I mean.

I remember entering my senior year at San Pedro High School in Southern California. My mom and dad were asked to come to the counselor's office for a conference. The school had just finished a battery of tests that would forever stamp each student with their IQ. You know that such visits are not always very positive. That day is still vivid to me.

I remember the gray 12-inch linoleum tiles on the floor, the pale green walls and the navy suit and white shirt worn by the counselor. I was sitting there, scared to death. I heard the counselor inform my parents that I would not be able to make it in college because my IQ score was so low. (The experts at that time were saying low IQ scores in high school were a sure sign of failure in college.) The counselor continued, "Marsha must develop skills so she will be employable after high school. Her schedule for the senior year should be changed to typing and office skills rather than college prep."

I was devastated. With my poor attitude, I thought, "Well fine. I've got a boyfriend. I'll just get married." I was a 16-year-old, an immature, wild and crazy girl.

Nurture your mind with great thoughts; to believe in the heroic makes heroes.

✦ *Disraeli*

I remember Dad saying, "No one is going to tell my daughter what she can or can't do. If she fails out, she will do it all on her own!" Thanks to my dad's insistence – along with bribery – I went on to college. Bribery – what a great motivator. My dad bribed me with $100 and said if I was still in love after one semester, I would have his blessing to marry. In less than a semester, I realized the importance of college. By the way, the $100 bought my textbooks.

In 1968, I graduated with my bachelor of arts degree in home economics with a biology minor from California State University at Long Beach. The weird major and minor came from changing my major so many times, failing organic chemistry, and basically having a tough time keeping focused. After four years, I went to my counselor and said, "With all the classes I've taken, what major can I claim to graduate in one year?" He replied, "With a home economics major and a biology minor, you will be able to teach school."

Notice that this education took five years instead of four. It wasn't easy. During my last year, studying elementary education, I discovered that I am partially dyslexic. Had we only recognized this learning disability in high school! (If you want more information on people succeeding with learning disabilities or dyslexia, read *Success, It can be yours!* by Terri Bowerstock.)

The negative experiences in high school could have changed my life. The difficult times in college could have changed my life. I didn't know it then, but these events helped me move closer to becoming the CEO of my life.

One support group deserves mention: In 1965, during my junior year of college, I joined Delta Delta Delta Sorority, the Phi Kappa chapter at Cal State Long Beach. The guiding

Wait
for
the
wisest
of all
counselors,
time.
✦ *Pericles*

support and encouragement I received from my sorority sisters, chapter leaders and national directors were wonderful. I was a party animal and their code of ethics and graces steered me to a more successful route. This group helped me understand the responsibility I must take for my life – no one else was going to do it for me!

All the pomp and circumstance of the graduation ceremony made me one proud puppy! What support groups do you have? Are you really listening and weighing the great advice you receive from them?

Teaching school was my job of choice in 1968. I began substitute teaching kindergarten in Westminster School District. Bad choice. I hated teaching, and it wasn't the kids – it was the parents!

I remember one morning, the parent of the most rambunctious child in class came to me complaining, "You are ruining my child." I felt like saying, "Well you have done a pretty good job already!" I cried all the way to my classroom and all the way home. It was then that I decided to seek out other employment. Business might be a better choice, I thought. I had a good attitude about the change, but had a hard time finding a job.

I saw an ad in the *LA Times*: "Candy Girl wanted. Sell candy and demonstrate products in stores. Salary and benefits." I got the job at Candy Specialties, a company based in Los Angeles.

After one year, my sales were terrific, so I asked if I could be placed on commission like the other male sales representatives. "Oh, no," I was told. "We would never put girls on commission." So I asked for a company car. I had an excellent approach and reason. My reason was: In the candy business,

Victory
belongs
to the
most
persevering.
✦ *Napoleon*

sales reps carried two 15-pound cases filled with chocolate novelties. My 1965 VW Beetle had no air conditioning and the Bunny Ears and Santa Heads would melt into their bodies. My samples were deformed! I needed an air conditioned car. I approached the manager. He said, "NO! Only the men have company cars." My first husband then went to the company and talked to the "men" in charge, and convinced them I should have a company car and be on commission. I think of that event now and know I've "come a long way, baby!"

My attitude wavered a bit then, but my self-esteem was devastated. It confirmed that I was just a dumb old girl. Then one day, a gentleman from GTE Directories (GTD) saw me selling my goodies in a Long Beach delicatessen. He asked if I had ever thought about selling Yellow Pages. After the battery of interrogations (meaning interviews), my dear friend Bob Wenzel hired me in 1972 to be a T-Girl (selling Yellow Pages over the telephone).

Nine months into my job with GTD, my buddy Barbara Kelly was promoted to division manager and her position as trainer was open. Being a sales trainer was my dream job. I told my supervisor I was interested in the job and he said he would pass the word on. I was under the impression I would be interviewed. Weeks went by. I went to my manager again and he said, "Oh we didn't think you were serious. After all, your husband wouldn't let you travel."

Arrrgggghhh!!! This only confirmed my negative self-talk from high school days. I was saying to myself, "I'm not smart enough, and they've figured it out! Maybe they're right. Maybe my husband wouldn't let me!"

Long story short: I didn't let that negative self-talk get in the way. I interviewed for the trainer position and was

We must have strong minds, ready to accept facts as they are.

✦ *Harry Truman*

promoted from telephone sales to management as the western region sales trainer. Loved that position! I was the trainer for more than three years and was then promoted into many management jobs during my 15-year tenure with GTD.

What negative self-talk is holding you back? Is your self-talk preventing you from becoming the CEO of YOU?

Evaluate your self-talk

Because of the daily inputs from our environment, many of our thoughts are negative, especially when we slip out of our comfort zone. Many studies verify that 77 percent of the time we talk negatively to ourselves and make statements like:

"They won't listen."

"They don't care."

"What does it matter?"

"I can't."

"It will never work."

"I can't change."

"My changing won't affect anything."

"I could have."

"I should have."

"I might have."

In trying to determine where these negatives come from, Susan Baile (*Building Self Esteem in your Child*) followed 3-year-old children around daily to see what kind of input they were exposed to. In 12 months, she found that on average, these children heard negative inputs and responses 432 times per day! I am sad to report that these same children experienced only 13 positive inputs per day.

Day after day, month after month, year after year, such negative inputs build a very negative shell around our lives.

Women
are
never
stronger
than
when they
arm
themselves
with
their
weakness.

✧ *Marie du Vichy-Chamrond,*
Marquis du Deffond

Think what it means when the first word children learn is *"No!"* Have you ever heard a parent say any of these to a child: *Be quiet; sit down; not now; you can't* and so on? Such statements, repeated hundreds of times a day, create negative thinking and poor self confidence.

Now think about your own self-talk – the ongoing chatter in your head. We all naturally develop an ongoing personal narrative that suffuses everything we experience. The bad news is that our first learnings tend to be cast in such a negative environment. The good news is that we can transform the negative personal talk into more positive statements to ourselves – if we so choose.

How will you know if you are talking negatively to yourself? Record your voice. Yes. Record your own voice. Place a small tape recorder next to the telephone, either at work or at home. Record the next half-dozen conversations you have – just your voice, not the other person's. Then take a quiet moment to listen to the tape. Listen for the negative words – *can't, not, no, won't, shoulda, woulda, coulda.*

However many negatives you hear, understand that these words transfer over from your private self-talk to your out-loud verbal communications to another.

The negative words emerge from our thinking, so if you hear them, you are thinking them. They contribute to the hardening of the attitude.

Choose just one word you hear frequently and work on changing that word for a more positive frame of reference. This is not easy. (Most people have a very negative attitude when they hear their own voice, often saying to themselves, "I hate my voice!" But how else will you know how your attitude is being communicated to others?)

Up
to a
certain
point
every
man is
what
he
thinks
he
is.
⬦ *F.H. Bradley*

One phrase to listen for is the *"Yabit Habit."* We begin many sentences with "Yes, but" and when said often enough, turns into the *Yabit Habit.* Such behavior directly relates to how we think to ourselves and talk to others.

People with the *Yabit Habit* turn others off because they are saying, "I don't agree with you." Changing this negative thinking helps us take a more optimistic approach to everything – including other people and their differences.

Rewards of an attitude of gratitude

- *You are comfortable with your communication skills* – Speaking and being heard is easy and comfortable for you because you have honed your communication skills by practicing. No matter what the situation is, you take an optimistic outlook.

- *Having a plan is easier when you apply the steps of goal setting* – You understand that "if it's meant to be it's up to me," and that if life is going to be better in five years, you are in charge. You gratefully realize you are in charge. There will be failures but you cannot succeed unless you take risk. Part of the downside of risk is failure. You are moving, and it's not backward!

- *Change is energizing* – Life is dynamic and change must be embraced. Growing your knowledge helps you accept your changing environment. You realize that knowledge builds wealth. Good relationships, the willingness to learn, job satisfaction, balance between work and home: all bring wealth to your life.

- *You are in control* – No longer do people push your buttons and get you bent out of shape. Staying in control allows you to be a better negotiator and helps

A
man
who
is
"of sound
mind"
is
one who
keeps
the
inner
madman
under lock
and
key.
⬧ *Paul Valery*

you persuade people to make appropriate decisions. You rarely stoop to their level of anger.

- *You are assertive* – You stand up for your rights without violating others' rights. You can say no without feeling guilty or losing your job. You ooze credibility, composure and confidence.
- *A kind word builds relationships* – Complimenting another sincerely is second nature. You build on the relationship by adding to the emotional bank account – yours and theirs.
- *You relate your talents confidently* – You are proud of what you have achieved and will share those successes when appropriate. You are interested in others' talents, and will often turn the conversation to their successes and strengths rather than yours.
- *You are a magnet in attracting positive, assertive people* – Your optimistic and realistic outlook attracts people with similar views. You accept that negative people rarely like your stance, but have learned that a network serves you better when it is filled with successful, forward-thinking people.

If you continue to do what you've always done, you'll continue to get what you've always got. Do you know people who expect life to be better and different in five years but are unwilling to do anything about it? Some people do not understand that life is not a spectator sport. If you want things to be better and different, you have to *do* something differently.

Non-participation gives us hardening of the attitude. Life goes on, and if we do not participate, life still goes on. If a negative attitude is not getting us where we want to go, then

Mediocre minds usually dismiss anything which reaches beyond their own understanding.

✧ *Francois de La Rochefoucauld*

why not change the attitude? Reshaping attitudes is possible. Awareness is the key initial step.

Attitude truly is everything

Here is a wonderful story from my friend Kay. Her friend Roger was the kind of guy you love to hate. He was always in a good mood and always had something positive to say. When someone would ask him how he was doing, he would reply, "If I were any better, I'd be twins!"

Roger was a unique manager and a natural motivator. Several salespeople had followed along with him as he was promoted around town from store to store. The reason? His attitude. If an employee was having a bad day, Roger always found a way of telling the employee how to look on the positive side of the situation.

Seeing this style really made Kay curious, so one day she asked Roger, "I don't get it. You can't be a positive person all of the time. How do you do it?"

Roger replied, "Each morning I wake up and say to myself, 'Roger, you have two choices today. You can choose to be in a good mood or in a bad mood.' I choose to be in a good mood. Each time something bad happens, I can choose to be a victim or I can choose to learn from it. I choose to learn from it. Every time someone comes to me complaining, I can choose to accept their complaining or I can point out the positive side of life. I choose the positive side of life."

"Yeah, right, but it's not that easy," Kay protested. "Yes it is," Roger said. "Life is all about choices. When you cut away all the externals, every situation is a choice. You choose how you react to situations. You choose how people will affect your mood. You choose to be in a good mood or bad mood. The bottom line: It's your choice how you live life."

It is the
understanding
that sees and hears;
It is the
understanding
that improves
everything,
that orders
everything,
and that acts,
rules, and
reigns.
⋄ *Epicharmus*

Several years later, Kay heard that Roger did something you are never supposed to do in a retail business: He left the back door open one morning and was held up at gunpoint by three armed robbers. While trying to open the safe, his hand, shaking from nervousness, slipped off the combination. The robbers panicked and shot him several times at close range. Luckily, Roger was found relatively quickly and rushed to the hospital.

After 18 hours of surgery and weeks of intensive care, Roger was released from the hospital with fragments of the bullets still in his body. Kay saw him about six months after the shooting. When she asked him how he was, he replied, "If I were any better, I'd be twins. Wanna see my scars?"

Kay declined, but did ask him what had gone through his mind during the robbery. "The first thing that went through my mind was that I should have locked the back door," Roger replied. "Then, as I lay on the floor, I remembered that I had two choices: I could choose to live or I could choose to die. I chose to live."

"Weren't you scared? Did you lose consciousness?" Kay asked.

Roger continued, "The paramedics were great. They kept telling me I was going to be fine. But when they wheeled me into the emergency room and I saw the expressions on the faces of the doctors and nurses, I got really scared. In their eyes, I read, 'He's a dead man.' I knew I needed to take action."

"What did you do?"

"Well, there was a big, burly nurse shouting questions at me. She asked if I was allergic to anything. 'Yes,' I replied. The doctors and nurses stopped working as they waited for my reply. I took a deep breath and yelled, 'Bullets!' Over their laughter, I told them, 'I am choosing to live. Operate on me as if I am alive, not dead.'"

O Lord,
who
lends
me
life,
lend me
a
heart
replete
with
thankfulness.

❖ *Shakespeare*

Roger lived, thanks to the skill of his doctors, but also because of his amazing attitude. Every day we have the choice to live fully. We choose to have hardening of the attitude or an attitude of gratitude.

Attitude, after all, is everything.

You choose: Where are you now, and where do you want to be? Are you the CEO of YOU?

Symptoms of hardening of the attitude:

+ People don't understand you

+ You are caught in a rut

+ Any kind of change bothers you

+ You are a bully

+ You are a doormat

+ No time for compliments

+ You are boastful

+ Positive people seem to drift away from you

+ You find yourself often depressed and often full of doubt and worry

+ You can't sleep at night

+ Thinking about what you don't have has become the center of your thought process

+ People don't seem responsive when you talk about important events in your life

+ Gossip keeps you connected

+ There are so many things that are wrong and broken

Rewards of an attitude of gratitude:

+ You are comfortable with your communication skills

+ Having a plan is easier when you apply the steps of goal setting

+ Change is energizing

+ You are in control

+ You are assertive

+ A kind word builds relationships

+ You relate your talents confidently

+ You are a magnet in attracting positive people

+ Life is a bowl of cherries

+ You awake rested and re-energized

+ You are grateful for what you have

+ Being empathetic is critical in your communications

+ Gossip is hurtful

+ You are grateful for the life you have developed for yourself

Chapter 3
◆
Response+able = responsible

Think about the word "responsible."

What does it mean to you?

What if you were to understand "responsible" to mean "having the knowledge, skills, and tools to be able to make a response?"

You will bring much more joy to your work life when you are able to respond appropriately to any work situation with proven knowledge, increased skills, and yes, even a few simple tools to help you deal with your responsibilities.

These key elements are a must for taking responsibility:

◆ **Stay calm – They can't get your goat if you don't tell them where it's tied up – so hide your goat. Learn what the experts do to stay calm.**

◆ **Accept change – We make a conscious decision whether to accept the dynamics of life or stay stuck in a rut – to shift or drift. You can enhance your skills in the change game.**

◆ **Stay focused – When you choose to use a very specific process of goal setting, acting, and focusing – you can have it all. Three simple tools will help you.**

Hide your goat

Numerous studies show that people who cannot control their anger are at much greater risk of heart disease, diabetes and illness. You've heard these familiar refrains:

"You tick me off."

"You stress me out."

Footprints
on the
sands
of
time
are
not
made
by sitting
down.
✧ *Anonymous*

"Boy, am I mad."

"I'll show them."

"They get my goat."

"I'll let them know who's boss!"

How do you react when people try to get your goat? What do you say to them and to yourself? Do you lose it? Or do you keep your cool?

Think about it. When you decide to engage in the anger of the situation, you give your power and control to the other person. Do you really want to hand someone your head on a platter?

Instead, stay calm

My dad, Marshall Petrie, always told me that when I get angry, I am choosing not to stay calm. He'd finish with, "And the only person who really cares that you are upset is you. No one else cares – it's your choice!"

Do you want to be in control of your life and its outcomes? Then you must learn to control at least two emotions: frustration and anger. If you think you handle yourself well in such stress or anger situations, do something really scary: Ask a close friend to tell you honestly how you handle yourself. Tell them to be honest and be ready for the feedback.

Such knowledge enables you to stay calm, but you must want to apply these three easy steps to staying calm:

Step 1 – Take a deep breath

Step 2 – Take a mental time-out

Step 3 – Switch to left-brain thinking

Step 1 – Take a deep breath

Can you feel yourself losing it? That's the moment when you slip into the fight or flight syndrome. Your breathing

There are
two
ways
of
spreading
light;
to
be the
candle
or
the
mirror
that
reflects
it.

⋄ *Edith Wharton*

changes because your body is readying itself to fight or flee. When you let people get your goat, you actually breathe more shallowly – you begin to pant and only about 20 percent of the oxygen you need is making its way to the brain. Eighty percent of your blood vessels are in your lower lungs. These blood vessels absorb oxygen from the air and transport it to your brain so you can think more clearly.

When you take a deep breath, you'll have the oxygen your brain needs to respond rather than react. Responding is a learned behavior; reacting comes naturally and usually lowers you to the other person's level.

Note: Women are different. Five UCLA researchers studied fight or flight and found that in some cases, women react differently when they become angry. Because many women have been socialized to be caregivers and nurturers, they want to find and fix the problem. The new term therefore is "tend and mend" for such women. And because most passive people hate conflict and will do anything to avoid it, the anger and conflict is held within themselves.

Use this breathing technique – 8+8+8: Eight seconds to draw the breath in through your nose, eight seconds to hold the breath, then eight seconds to exhale.

If that feels like a long time to you, put one hand on your stomach and feel the air slowly filling that lower space down deep in your lungs. Visualize the air entering your body: clean, clear and crystal blue. Hold your breath for eight seconds to allow the blood vessels in the lungs to absorb the oxygen. Then exhale steadily through the nose.

Visualize this released air leaving your body: brown and green, a toxic waste dripping with slime and foam. All those ugly emotional toxins are being released with your exhaled breath.

Troubles
are often
the
tools
by which
God
fashions
us for
better
things.
❖ *H.W. Beecher*

Repeat if needed.

You can turn this 8+8+8 breathing technique into a wonderful negotiating ploy. Expert negotiators say to watch another's body language, especially their breathing. Are their shoulders heaving up and down? Does their breathing look labored? These are usually signs of improper breathing. So now you are in control because they are not! This is a great example of learning how to respond rather than how to react.

Step 2 – Take a mental time-out

You can do this when you begin Step 1. Taking a time-out serves us well in anger because we should pause to think anyway, instead of immediately trying to solve the problem. A mental time-out allows us time to regroup and refocus – just as sports teams take a time-out to review their game plan and refocus on the objective of the next action. So regroup your thoughts and refocus your attention while you count 8+8+8 slowly to yourself as you inhale, hold, and exhale.

Step 3 – Switch to left-brain thinking

The right brain is the creative and innovative side of our thinking. This is also the side where fear lives. We have negative voices (I call them "mental terrorists") talking to us 77 percent of the time – especially when we are dealing with someone we don't understand, their background, their accent, their views. Your right brain can create a negative environment for you, so you need to learn to manipulate your own thinking.

As you know, the left brain is very structured and linear. It is also where we form words. If you memorize and store some words that you can quickly pull out of your left brain toolbox, you will better manage the situation and thus stay in control! So here's the mantra:

In all
troublous
events
we may
find
comfort,
though
it be
only
in the
negative
admission
that
things
might
have
been
worse.

⟡ *Barr*

This is a test. Only a test. This will not be important in 10 years.

Better yet, make that 100 years, suggests Dr. Richard Carlson, author of *Don't Sweat the Small Stuff Because It's All Small Stuff.* In a hundred years it really won't be important – because then you won't even be here!

Add this mantra to your toolbox, so you can respond, not react. Responding is learned, reacting is not. It's like taking a medication. If you respond – that's good. You get well. If you react – that's not so good! Your medication will have to change. Better to respond, not react.

Then, no matter what happens, you will be ready to use your personal power. Remember this little fact, too: It takes approximately two hours to calm down and refocus after you get frustrated and angry. What a great time management tool!

A final note: Gender differences in how we handle anger abound. Men tend to be hotheaded blowups, whereas women sometimes suffer in silence. Researchers at Southwest Missouri State University found that these differences need some explaining. Dr. Deborah Cox, the study's co-author and professor of counseling at SMSU says, "Men feel more effective when they express their anger outwardly; women generally feel that their anger is counterproductive and try not to show it."

The belief that anger is unladylike keeps many women from openly expressing frustration, Cox says, but it does not stop them from dealing with it. "When the occasion calls for it, women often act on their anger regardless of their comfort level, but they may find ways to assert themselves that don't involve talking openly about their anger." In other words, women really solve the anger problem the same as men. They just don't let everyone in the room hear about it.

It is
not
designed
that
the
road
should be
made
too
smooth
for us
here
upon
earth.
✦ *Jane Porter*

Shift or drift

The second key element for taking responsibility is to make a conscious choice to accept change. You either shift or drift: You can decide to shift with the changing dynamics of life, or you can decide to let someone else run your life – and you then just drift. Successful people make the choice to shift and thereby manage themselves in their constantly changing environment.

Making the choice to shift (and therefore change) is difficult. Do you know people who want to shift from where they are, but just can't? Without shifting, the road to success is muddied, filled with potholes and detours. The path we choose to take leads us either to be a success or a loser.

I've learned there are always three choices, and when I get stuck on the path or reluctant to change to a new road, I back myself out of the corner and say, "OK, kid! You've got three choices, you can:

- ✦ **ACCEPT it.**
- ✦ **LEAVE it.**
- ✦ **CHANGE it.**

Accepting the situation as it currently stands is often a good choice, because we've set a goal with a strategy to create a future we want to be different. Accepting it as it is means you won't be stressed out because you have thought through the possibilities and you are in control. You have a plan, so you know the future you want.

Leaving an undesired situation is the hardest choice. You or people you know may have left a job because their goals or company's direction were against their values, precepts or principles. Or you may have left a relationship because the

Troubles,
like babies,
grow
large
by
nursing.
✧ *Lady Holland*

partner was physically or mentally abusive – or maybe both. I had to leave my first marriage because the trust was gone, and I knew I was not going to change the other person.

Changing it may have some risk: The most common reason people don't change is because they do not have confidence in their decisions – whether from poor choices in the past, lack of self-esteem, or little faith in themselves.

We've all met people who do not like to be reminded of these choices, and you'll hear it in their language: "I can't accept the way things are. Look at the way my boss treats me! He treats me like dirt and I not taking it any more! (Pause) But you know, I can't leave. I have to have the money. I can't give up the benefits. And besides, how could I change anything there? Are you kidding? I'm just a little old fish in a great big pond. They'll never listen to me, anyway!"

I call such people victims, or maybe witless martyrs. They do not take responsibility for their lives. Remember, if you continue to do what you've always done, you'll continue to get what you've always got. There are no miracles in life. People are not lucky in life. They work hard for what they want – and they get it.

I made a choice quite a few years ago. I looked around at people who had taken charge of their lives to create what they wanted. I saw that they became active participants in shaping their lives. I learned that we can do whatever we want, and that it's not that we can't, but rather that we choose not to.

Life is not a spectator sport. We cannot sit on the sidelines and expect our dreams to come true. The only magic wand is held by us: We create magic in our lives out of continued focus, discipline, and making better choices tomorrow than maybe we did today.

If a
friend
is in
trouble,
don't
annoy him
by
asking
if there
is anything
you can
do.
Think
up
something
appropriate
and
do it.

⋄ *Edgar*
Watson
Howe

I am often surprised at the comments I receive on the evaluation cards after one of my presentations. I understand that "the boss" sends many people to hear motivational speakers like me. But what do you make of this comment? *"I expected the seminar to help me in my work, not as a person."*

You can readily think of at least two interpretations of such a statement. It may be "magic wand thinking": Give me some magical tools to apply at work, because I am not really interested in changing as a person. Or, positively: Any tool I use at work directly correlates to my growth as a person.

Positive motivation

Choosing to shift rather than drift comes from motivation. Some people engage in lottery thinking. Yes, one in a million do win – but can you hold your breath till then? So I've learned, finally, that to really enjoy success you have to be both positive and motivated.

The key: Every morning when you wake up, you have the choice to be positive (optimistic) or negative (pessimistic).

Have you ever gotten up in the morning and said to yourself, "I just don't feel like it!" Maybe it's your job or your life. You feel like pulling the covers over your head and hiding from the world through more sleep.

Most people find that first hour of each day to be the most critical and the most beneficial. I've learned to jump, yes, jump out of bed and welcome the day. If I am feeling blue, I get myself in front of a mirror and 10 times say to myself, "I like myself, I like myself, I like myself...." (I recommend you do this in the privacy of your home or people will think you are ready for the rubber room.) If you don't believe your self-talk, no one else will.

Some
people are
so
fond
of ill luck
that
they run
halfway
to
meet it.
✦ *Douglas
William Jerrold*

Your morning choice, of course, has tremendous impact on your personal and professional life. What do you choose to do? Here's a quick quiz for you. Answer yes or no:

I am responsible for my attitude.

I am responsible for my focus and discipline.

I am responsible for my choices.

Of course you know the answers. You know you are the responsible party.

You can have it all

Have you ever made some New Year's resolutions, only to look back at the end of the year to find them long untouched and unfulfilled? Do you ever have really good intentions, but the real action to implement them never takes place? Many of us have set these annual, monthly or daily targets, only to find that at the end of the year we have completely forgotten about the goals. And when you reflect seriously, you say, "Wow, those were pretty good. What happened?"

We lost focus and our actions were driven by someone or something else – a parent, partner, boss, peer, friend, subordinate or superior. We allow this to happen because it's easy to become a little lazy. And it's so much easier to play by someone else's rules than our own. We easily fall into the illusion that there's a big group out there called "they" and "them," whose sole job is to judge us harshly for our failures:

"Oh no, if I set a goal and I don't achieve it, what will they say?" "I was warned that this was going to be hard, and they were right."

When we stop setting goals and focusing on what we want, our risk muscle begins to atrophy. Achieving goals and getting anything you want takes risk and often failure.

If I
try
to be
like
him,
who
will be
like
me?

✧ *Yiddish*
proverb

If you are not failing, you are not moving ahead.

The goal-setting process

Here is a specific process for setting goals. I have found that it works:

1. Write your goal as an affirmation.
2. Create an action plan.
3. Keep focused.

Step 1 – Write your goal as an affirmation

Rather than saying, "some day I hope to be," or "I wish this would change," tell yourself instead that the goal has already been achieved. "I am the successful manager of my department." "We have resolved this conflict and are working together harmoniously now." You thus use affirmative "I am" language to create a positive focus for your goals.

Negative self-talk is so debilitating. When you say you can't, won't be able to, it'll never work – you really begin to believe it.

Have you heard about the studies that clearly show how some children follow their parents' dependence on welfare even to the third and fourth generation? Welfare has become their goal, though usually not consciously. Some are no longer even counted as unemployed. Not only have they dropped off the screen; they have been trained to the expectation of having someone take care of them.

Thomas Sowell, syndicated newspaper columnist, is a great example of breaking away from such an expectation. He not only had the drive and the focus, but loving parents who were not abusing drugs or alcohol. His parents celebrated his seventh-grade graduation because he was the first one to

To really
enjoy
the better
things
in
life,
one must
first
have
experienced
the
things
they are
better
than.
⬩ *Oscar Holmolka*

make it that far in school! They were proud and gave him love, encouragement, kindness and, most of all, hope.

He tells about a friend taking him on his first trip to a library as a youngster. His pal had to tell him what a library was and how to use it. Thomas was amazed that this place, filled with all these books, had enough trust in you to let you take books home!

How simple a trip to the library may seem – but not to Thomas Sowell. It changed his life. What has changed your life? What will change your life?

Here is a personal example: In 1990, I set a goal and, of course, wrote it as an affirmation: "I am married to the man of my dreams by my 50th birthday." I had been divorced for 18 years. Knowing that another of my goals was to retire by 50, I wanted someone special to share my life with – a soul mate.

I reasoned that with my longevity genes, I would probably live to be at least 100, so the possibility of living another 50 years or so is quite good! One of my friends said, "You have a goal to remarry? Have you noticed that you don't pick men well? Hey, I think your picker is broken." She was absolutely right. So I asked for a suggestion. Immediately she said, "In your action plan, write this: Join a dating service." I am thinking to myself – NO WAY! The thought of joining a dating service and marketing myself made my skin crawl. So step No. 2 is –

Step 2 – Develop an action plan

When I wrote my goal of being married to the man of my dreams, I had just moved from Atlanta to Phoenix. I knew no one in town. I also realized that before you marry, it's a good idea to date first and go shopping for Mr. Right.

Resolve
to be thyself;
and
know
that he
who
finds
himself,
loses his
misery.
✧ *Matthew Arnold*

As a professional female, meeting someone to spend the rest of my life with was problematic: Dating men related to my professional life was considered corporate suicide at that time. Yet two friends from my home state, California, had enlisted in a dating service with great success.

One was now married and the other was very serious. Both found men that were outstanding, and not video rejects. My skepticism for video dating was, however, still intact.

With plan A down the tubes, and plan B (the singles group at church) a total flop, I was quickly driven to plan C – the dreaded dating service.

One afternoon while sitting at my desk and feeling very sorry for myself, I decided it was time to get a life. I picked up the Yellow Pages and flipped to Dating Service. This really was the last resort, the bottom of the barrel, the pits! But I remembered the success of my California friends, so I thought, what the heck!

One ad attracted attention: "Exclusively for the professional." I called and they quickly hooked me.

After a few dates (I use the term loosely) another videotape arrived. Having become fairly skeptical and suspicious, I opened my other mail first, poured myself a glass of wine, changed clothes, and finally decided to see what this one looked like.

He was too good to be true! Soon I had a phone conversation with Al Sue. Truly – a boy named Sue!

We had our first coffee in February, dated as much as our careers would allow, and were engaged in July. We were married the day after Thanksgiving. We joked, "Well, we're just a couple of turkeys finally getting together."

Was it a risk? You bet!

Am I glad a flexed my risk muscle? You bet!

We grow weary of those things (and perhaps soonest) which we most desire.

⬧ *Samuel Butler*

Now I am often asked about using a dating service. Here is some of my personal advice.

- Are there additional charges for changing your initial video?
- Make sure you edit the "resume" or video they use for you.
- How many videos can you expect to receive within a month?
- How many men or women are currently enrolled within your age group?
- Check references: Talk to couples they have matched.
- What is the average time to find a match?
- Do they sponsor events or have parties for members?
- Ask for evidence that they do have the kind of person you're seeking.
- Stay flexible and open . . . and have fun.

Step 3 – Keep focused

Have you ever set New Year's resolutions and not achieved them? Ever look back 12 months later and wonder why? The No. 1 reason is we have not taken responsibility for our actions on a day-to-day basis, month after month. At what point do you lose focus on your goals? Most people I have surveyed have admitted to losing sight of their goals within the first week of setting them. The reason? They begin working on other people's goals and forget to integrate their own goals to their activities.

The rules I have learned that force responsibility in focus include:

- Have fewer than 10 goals at any given time. Include your professional and personal goals and integrate them. This will provide balance in your life and your goals. Many people have business goals only – then when they achieve them, they wonder why they do not feel satisfied. They are out of balance because all energy has been on work.
- Read your goals at least weekly. Keep your objective in view. I'm amazed at how this works. I read my goals regularly to remind myself of what I still need to do.

The
man
who goes
farthest
is generally
the
one
who
is willing to
do
and
dare.

The sure thing
boat
never gets far
from
the
shore.

✦ *Dale Carnegie*

A good example of how this works relates to listening to music in your car. You are humming along on the road, following the songs on the radio. The last tune you hear remains in your mind for the day. Every time your mind wanders, you find yourself humming the same tune. The song permeates your thinking.

When we review our goals on a regular basis, our unconscious mind keeps reminding us of our targets. I can take the responsibility of applying these thoughts to my actions. When I choose an action, I ask myself, "Is this going to move me closer or farther away from my goal?" This is the best time management tool I use on a regular basis:

+ **Follow up on your goal work by visualizing your success. Picture exactly how it will look when you achieve the feat. How will you feel? What will your thoughts be? What will people say to you? How will you look? Think of it all.**

+ **Establish a realistic deadline. Allow flexibility. If you need to push a date to a more realistic time frame, do it! This enables you to live with the unexpected delays of life. Ask yourself if the delay is self-inflicted, or is it because you were pushing yourself a little too hard? Evaluate every date that changes, and each goal you achieve.**

I have always wanted to do volunteer work in politics. Women's issues are also very important to me. Because I have the ability to deliver a significant message in both of these areas, I wanted to find something that would help me meet this goal. The WISH List has been my answer – Women In the Senate and House. The entire focus of this group is to elect more women to the House and Senate. When I learned that the United States ranks with third world countries in the number of women in politics, I decided WISH was the ticket.

The more
we
do,
the more
we
all
can do; the
more
busy
we are,
the more
leisure
we have.
⋄ *Hazlitt*

What are your wishes and dreams? What do you really want out of life? The answer cannot be, "I just want to be happy, or I want to be successful." Success and happiness have different meanings for different people.

When I talk about success in workshops, often people will ask, "What is success?" For me, success is having good health, continuing to build a loving relationship with my husband and having the financial ability to do what we want.

Happiness is seeing the elation Al has when I do something out of my comfort zone and succeed. On a recent camping trip, I quizzed him on the way home, "What was your favorite part of our time in the woods?" He stopped, contemplated and, as only Al can explain, "Knowing that you experienced and enjoyed something that is one of my passions – the outdoors." I am responsible and response+able for his reply and that thrills me.

Set goals. Determine what worked and what did not along the path of success. Change, be flexible, move with courage and be accepting of challenges. Take responsibility for you. Are you willing? Are you able? Are you response+able?

Never
put off till
tomorrow
what you
can do
today.

You may enjoy
doing
so much
that you
want
to do it
again.

⬧ *Ross Perot*

Chapter 4

✦

Human doing or human being?

Are you in control of your time so you can live your life as a human being? Or is time controlling you so you have become a human doing? Are you so busy doing this and that for other people, but never have time for yourself?

I was a human doing for a very long time: Doing errands for my mother, friends and family; doing my job 10 hours a day, six days a week or more; doing favors that were outside of my work objectives for peers at work and my boss. Of course, such stress affected my health.

Have you ever felt so unbalanced over the lack of time that you are totally torn between home and work? You know you need to spend more time with your family and friends, but your job has become so demanding that you barely have time to drive home, shower, and pass out in bed. And when you are at work, the constant pull of being asked to do more with less is overwhelming.

The stress created from feeling out of control is making you physically sick, upset and cranky. You run like a hamster on an endless wheel, jumping from one ring to the next, only to find out the rings are on fire and you get burned. Is this the endless trek of a human doing?

There is one constant for all human beings: We all have 24 hours each day. No one has more time or less time than the next person. We all have exactly the same number of minutes from sunup to sundown.

We can
do
anything
we want
to do if we
stick
to it
long
enough.
✦*Helen Keller*

So why then do some people seem so well organized while others run around like the proverbial headless chicken? Short answer: They take their role of human being very seriously. They are selfish with their time; they carefully manage every day of their existence; and they delegate. Here's how they learn to live like a human being:

- *Pick and choose:* Until we learn how to prioritize what to do first, and what will give us the best results, we will suffer the do-it-all syndrome. Being overwhelmed is a choice. Simply put, we choose not to manage our time.
- *Time impediments:* Neutralize procrastination and control interruptions. The simple truth is: We all procrastinate, and such behavior can wipe out all good intentions. The main reason we delay making decisions is fear. Why put off for tomorrow what you can do today? Who knows, you might like it so much that you want to do it again! And did you know that every time you are interrupted, you spend about eight minutes getting your focus back to where it was when you left off? The ability to say "yes" to decisions and "no" to needless interruptions is critical.
- *Build people skills:* The better our relationship with other human beings, the less time it will take to get them to accept our ideas. Delegation is the key time-management skill. You cannot delegate well if you have poor relationships. Have you ever tried to delegate to someone who has an attitude?

Pick and choose

The most effective tool I use to prioritize is to take my to do list and ask myself, "Is there anything on this list that does not help me reach my goals?" If there is, I reevaluate the priority as

As
every
thread of
gold is
valuable,
so is
every
moment
of time.

❖ *J. Mason*

to its real importance. I ask, "If it doesn't get done, what will happen? Will I upset a client, miss a deadline, shut down a possible opportunity, miss valuable learning, or what?"

If an action is not going to move me closer to achieving a goal, then why do it? Remember, our lives encompass our professional and personal goals. This step of validating actions against goals is critical.

We should get to the point that we can review this process in our heads without even looking at our written goals. That's why goals should have both personal and professional targets. Not having goals spreads grease on the path of life, and we begin to slip backward. Soon we find ourselves at the bottom of a steep slope.

I have learned that good time management means keeping focused on what is important to success. First, you must determine what actions move you toward task completion. Depending on the particular situation, ask these two questions any time a new task appears on your to do list:

Estimated time – Is the time invested worth the expected outcome?

Visibility – Who will notice if it doesn't get done?

Of course you need discipline to ask these two questions. We often take on so many tasks automatically because saying "yes" has become habit. If the time you must invest is not worth the outcome, then stop yourself and ask: "Then why am I doing it?"

I take two approaches to prioritization. The first is the Comparison Game: Look at only the first two entries on your massive to do list. Ask, "If I have time to do only one of these, which one would I do?" Pretend you must leave the office in 10 minutes and have just this short period of time to

Well
arranged
time
is the surest
mark
of a
well arranged
mind.

✦ *Pitman*

get one task started. This game works well because you are limiting the decision to just two items, not your entire list.

If your task list is extensive, continue this process and ask yourself the comparison question again, this time looking at No. 3 on your to do list and comparing its importance to No. 1. Again ask, "If I have time to do just one, which one would I do?" Compare the first item with every other item on the list. I like to put a tick or check mark by the items I determine to be most important in my paired comparison.

Then I go back to item No. 2 and start all over again. If I have time to do just one, would I do No. 2 or No. 3? Then I compare No. 2 to No. 4. Each task is thus weighed against every task. A tick or check mark identifies which task to complete in a time crunch. The rank order is determined by adding up the check marks. Ties are broken by applying the same process. (If I had time to do just one, which one would I do?)

The Comparison Game is a quick and simple way to determine what to do first. Visibility, recognition, or cost factors come next. With your high-priority list in front of you, simply go down the list to evaluate the consequences of doing/not doing them.

Time impediments

The key to overcoming procrastination is discovering the reason behind it. I like what Zig Ziglar says: The common underpinning of procrastination is F-E-A-R.

F = False
E = Evidence
A = Appearing
R = Real

When
a
decision
has to be
made,
make it.
There is
no
totally
right time
for
anything.
✦ *General George Patton*

Let's look at F-E-A-R more closely:

False – Negative thinking can overwhelm you, reinforcing your belief of not having the skill, resources, gumption, or time to COMPLETE a project. So you don't even attempt to BEGIN it. The fear of failure becomes so overwhelming that starting a project never happens. You assume you are going to fail – even though you haven't even started. Result? You let something that never was get in your way.

I sometimes see examples of such negative thinking on the evaluation sheets turned in after one of my presentations on goal setting. One of my keynotes is called, "Go for the Gold." I discuss the process of changing your life. One of the questions on the evaluation form asks, "How will this information help you?" Some interesting responses:

"It won't help me at this time. I have too much to do now."

"My boss would never let me set goals."

"Great information, just not applicable to me."

But then I get responses from people who get it and are willing to move beyond their own fear and negative self-talk:

"Wonderful, life-changing presentation."

"Have been setting goals for years and understand now that my own negative thinking is getting in the way."

"Specific steps that when broken down, are doable!"

"Thanks, Marsha, for the recharging. Just what I needed."

"Accomplishing my wishes and dreams is my responsibility."

"I've learned that if it's meant to be it's up to me."

Where do you fit? Are you willing to put past failures and negative events behind you? My dad always said everything happens for a positive reason and it is our duty as humans to figure out what that learning is. The problem is often the unrealistic expectation of immediate gratification.

Fear
is the
Tax
that
conscience
pays
to
guilt.
✦ *Sewell*

Evidence – We may have so many failed attempts and experiences stored in our heads, we begin to believe we shouldn't even think about trying. This "evidence" is supported by failure. Our self-talk is saying, "What if you start and don't do it right? You will have to tell them why you failed." Such "evidence" is repeated and validated in school. If you did not do your homework right, you did not receive a good grade. In other words, you failed. You might have evidence that being passed up for promotion was only because the boss didn't like you! Well, there you are. Evidence in the flesh and blood.

The real evidence may be that in school I goofed around, didn't study or do my homework, so it showed in my test scores and grades. The real evidence of not receiving the promotion is that my conflict management skills are lacking, or my team loyalty isn't good, or my interpersonal skills need some polish. Real evidence is hard to accept because it means I am responsible for the evidence in my life.

Refocusing on the positive outcome rather than the negative result is the way out. Here are tips that work:

+ **Break the project down to its smallest common denominator.**
+ **Plan a reward.**
+ **Chart it out.**
+ **Begin with the easiest.**
+ **Begin anywhere.**
+ **Delegate a small part to create momentum.**

Appearing – We weaken ourselves. The procrastinated project appears to be so large, we talk ourselves into the failure belief. So we don't start at all! The lack of belief in ourselves overwhelms the positive thinking.

If I want to change that appearance, one of the first steps

In the end, thought rules the world. There are times when impulses and passions are more powerful, but they soon expend themselves; while mind, acting constantly, is ever ready to drive them back and work when their energy is exhausted.

⬩ *J. McCosh*

I take is to have the BELIEF in myself that I can succeed. I want to think confidently, which in turn comes out of my mouth as real and true.

Have you tried a Ben Franklin list lately? It's a list that accounts for all your strengths and weaknesses.

Here's how it works: Take a lined tablet and make two columns. Title the left side, "Talents and Capabilities," and the right side, "Could do Better."

I challenge you to do this for yourself. Become a human being, not a human doing. Mine looks a bit like this:

Talents and Capabilities	Could do Better
✦ Energy	✦ Minutiae involvement
✦ Focused	✦ Prioritize projects
✦ Take responsibility	✦ Communicate specific needs
✦ Interpersonal skills	✦ Follow up after delegation
✦ Anger management	✦ Not take things personally

The true belief we have in our own capabilities is how we change our thinking. True belief enables us to put aside the naysayers and hear their message for what it is. It may appear to be real, but after careful analysis, we see they are afraid, concerned, jealous, or envious of factors that are positive in us. But because of their own lack of self-confidence, they don't want us to succeed or even to try.

The secret here is to know who you really are – the capabilities you actually have, and not how they appear to be.

Real – When the same events result in negative outcomes, we mentally trap ourselves into thinking everything else that occurs will have the same results. Our thinking may seem REAL because of the past and what we view as current validation. Our brain is taught the "if – then" principle:

Thought
means
life,
since
those who
do not
think do not
live in any
high
or real
sense.

✦ *A.B. Alcott*

- **If I take a risk and fail, then people will think I'm a loser.**
- **If I change jobs and don't like it, then I will be sorry I left the old job.**
- **If I set goals and don't achieve them, then I'll be right where I am anyway.**
- **If I leave this relationship, then I may never find anyone else again.**

This is a real mind game we constantly play. I present workshops and keynotes on this exact topic – and I STILL catch myself falling into this mental trap. Regular review of such brain insanity will catch such flawed thinking. We must understand that these are only thoughts, not the actual occurrences or outcomes. The kicker here is that our fears become a self-fulfilling prophecy.

In studying unemployment and the cause of the ongoing issue of keeping people employed, I was surprised to find that some people are in total belief they can't find a job. If they did, (they think) then they would not have the skill to perform the job. If they can't do the job to expectations, then they will be fired. If they tried this job, it would be short-lived, so then they would be back on welfare. So if they don't even upset the system they are in, then they will have peace of mind.

Such "if – then" thinking weakens us. For the first time in the history of our country, we are getting into third, fourth and fifth generations on welfare. The modeling the children see while growing up becomes their expectation.

Are you willing to unlearn a thought that has become a barrier? Are you willing to relearn a new technique to move you to the next level that allows you to then become the CEO of YOU? One way is to challenge yourself with awareness: Write down one thought or belief that stands in the way of your success, then ask: What will I do to change such thoughts? Demand answers from yourself!

Success
covers
a
multitude
of
blunders.
H.W. Shaw

One more thought on procrastination

Creative procrastination – We know we are going to put tasks off – after all, we are human. So I now allow myself to procrastinate by doing it creatively! Here's how:

+ **Receive a project or assignment.**
+ **Scan it cover to cover.**
+ **Put it in a file folder.**
+ **Arrgghh! The deadline is fast approaching!**
+ **You complete the project in time!**

Our brains are very powerful. By scanning the project, issue, or problem the moment it hits my desk, I am planting the seed in my mind. Our brains are more powerful than we give them credit for. We use less than 2 percent of our brain.

The scanned input ferments in our minds. The subconscious begins planning, strategizing, asking relevant questions (even setting up meetings) so when the time crunch is upon us, we have already begun, without doing so consciously.

The tendency is to receive a project, be overwhelmed with the title or size of it, and put it aside because of being overwhelmed! Then the big moment is upon us! We have no clue to the contents of the project, no idea of the intricacies involved, no indication of who can help. And there we are, crazy once more, because we have become, yet again, a human doing instead of a human being! What are you willing to put in place before the next onslaught of work?

Control interruptions

Besides procrastination, the other time impediment is the inability to control interruptions.

I am not suggesting the total elimination of interruptions, only your control of them. Effective time management means

Too
many
failures
are
traced
to a lack
of
persistence
and not lack of
talent
or
ability.

⬧ *Dr. Paul Parker*

you can start one project and work as long as you can on it, then switch. Constant interruptions prevent such focus. Researchers at the University of Michigan studied the Miller Mutual Life Insurance Company and found that one hour of quiet time (no interruptions) can increase productivity by 27 percent. This is why many arrive an hour early or stay an hour late, because there are no interruptions.

Here is another time eater: people interruptions and self interruptions. Every time you are interrupted, either by someone else or by yourself, it typically takes eight minutes to refocus to the depth of thinking and concentration you had before the interruption.

People interruptions

When people enter your office, ask how you can help them. Eliminate "How are you?" (Most of the time you'll hear more than you care to know.)

Instead, be assertive. For example, tell your guest you are in the middle of a project and will have time for them either at 3 p.m. or 4:30 p.m. Ask, "Which time is better for you?"

Set ground rules. Establish quiet time for yourself. Retraining others can take time, because you may have allowed interruptions for so long. Co-workers are in the habit of interrupting because you have frequently given them approval to do so!

Stand up. When a co-worker enters your domain, stand up. Most people will want to establish eye contact, so standing up usually keeps them from sitting down. If they don't leave, begin moving slowly and step toward the entrance of your office. Again, let eye contact do the work for you. They will follow you! Then continue this by walking them back to their office. Veteran interrupters will suddenly look around and ask themselves, "How did I get here?"

Men
do not
fail;
they
give up
trying.

✦ *Root*

Self interruptions

When someone enters your office and quietly places something new in your in basket, do you feel compelled to snatch it up to see what it is? Self interruption. It's better to have a semi-scheduled time to retrieve new materials from your in basket.

You hear your computer beep, announcing a new e-mail. You MUST flip around in your chair to see what is there. Self interruption again – and it just cost you eight more minutes! Rather, establish time periods designated for reading and answering e-mail.

Consolidate tasks when possible. You can thus easily pick up an extra five minutes a day this way. Your payback? You'll gain 22 hours more per year – almost three more working days! What could you do with that extra time?

Build people skills

The better your relationship with other human beings, the less time it takes to get them to accept your ideas. You cannot delegate well if you have poor relationships. Have you ever tried to delegate to someone who has an attitude? This becomes time consuming and debilitating as you try to rise above human doing toward human being. Delegation is your key time-management skill and probably the most overlooked. Approach delegation with a positive attitude, rather than dwelling on whatever happened in the past.

The keys to delegation are not complex. If you miss one of these six skills of delegation, you will certainly provoke a negative outcome. You cannot wrap the delivery of delegation in sarcasm, rolling eyes or closed body language. If you really want a positive outcome, speak from your heart.

There
are
few
who have
at once
thought
and capacity
for
action.
Thought
expands,
but lames;
action
animates,
but narrows.
⋄ *Goethe*

- *Expectation* – First, tell the person what you want – the objective, target, or expected outcome – in a specific and detailed manner.
- *Confirmation* – Eliminate "Do you understand?" This statement creates a negative environment and often will put one on the defensive. Why not use something like this: "I want to make sure I explained this properly, so could you please play it back in your own words?" You seek confirmation of what they heard, through their own word filters. Here is where expected outcomes are often missed – you assume they got it, but they really didn't. If you are the one being delegated to, use the confirmation request in reverse: "So what you're asking me to do is…"
- *Deadline* – This gives people some ownership in the process. When possible, ask the other person for a reasonable deadline. If it's not what you want, negotiate with them. Find out why there are differences, so you can overcome unknown barriers or lack of resources.
- *Let them try it their way!* Oh, scary. You may feel a shiver moving down your spine at the thought of this, but why not let them try? They may have a better approach, new thoughts, or creative applications not thought of by you or others. This can save both time and money.
- *Follow up* – Always let the person know how they did. Please do not descend to a "shoulda, coulda, woulda" scolding, which creates a poor attitude. Instead, use the "liked best, next time" technique: Find one thing they did well and tell them that first. THEN tell them what to change next time. You are guaranteed one thing – you cannot change what has occurred. But what you can

I wasted
time, and
now
. doth
time
waste
me.
✦ *Shakespeare*

change is the result you get next time. Follow-up creates a better relationship and sets the stage for further positive delegation.

- *Give credit where credit is due* – If they have done a good job, let them know and let others know! Share the spotlight, the accolades, and the recognition.

We make choices every day on whether we are a human being or a human doing. What are your choices?

I encourage you to circle one idea you will explore for the rest of this week:

Prioritize – What technique will you use to prioritize your next overwhelming to-do list?

Procrastination – Which approaches will help you overcome procrastination? Do you understand F-E-A-R (False Evidence Appearing Real)? Do you react or respond? How will you control your interruptions?

Build People Skills – Name two persons you will practice the six skills of delegation on, and identify to positive expected results.

Welcome, human being!

There is
not a
single
moment
in life
that
we
can
afford
to lose.

✦ *Goulburn*

Chapter 5

✦

Unsafe stress

Have you ever noticed how some people can experience the same situation as another, yet one is calm and the other crazed? The calm person has learned to view stress as a learning laboratory that they visit on a regular basis, whether they want to or not. They learn from each stressful event.

When I was working at GTEDC, I applied for a promotion to the National Sales Division. I was told the company never placed women in National Sales and, besides, my husband wouldn't want me to travel. Mad is an understatement! I was furious! Angry! Stressed!

My dad helped me bring this event into focus. He asked, "What did you learn?" Upon reflection, I decided:

+ **I had to become an independent, positive thinker in the business world.**
+ **I had to be better than others (both men and women) so my work would be noticed.**
+ **I had to improve my networking skills.**
+ **I had to learn to control anger and remind myself to –**
   Think before I speak
   Practice speaking the truth
   Know when to keep quiet
   Refuse to partake in gossip
   Stop wasting time with fools
   Avoid the temptation to argue
   Refuse to speak negatively

It is
good
to rub and
polish
our brain
against
that of
others.
✦ *Montaigne*

Stress means different things to different people. Here are some of the ways people identify stress. How do you identify with stress?

Feelings	**Lifestyle**
Dissatisfaction	**Intensive drive**
Anxiety	**Aggressiveness**
Apprehension	**Time management**
Depression	**Impatience**
Sadness	**Guilty when not busy**
Events	**Symptoms**
Death of family member	**Ulcers**
Divorce	**Migraines**
Separation	**Hypertension**
Business failure	**Heart attack**
Parenting	**Headaches**
Loss of job	**Stroke**

Homework story

George is married and has two children, ages 3 and 5. His relationship with his wife is deteriorating because he is spending more and more time at work with projects, clients and emergencies. His children are growing up quickly and he is feeling guilty because he is missing out on their development. He knows going back to school will be necessary for his next promotion, but he hasn't found the time to enroll.

His daily routine is overwhelming. He gets up at 5 a.m. to play racquetball at the YMCA with his buddy. He showers at the Y, grabs a fast-food breakfast, and rushes to work. He must be on call for his demanding boss and clients who often wait until the last half hour of the day to bring emergency projects to his

All bitter
feelings
are
avoided,
or at least
greatly
reduced
by prompt,
face-to-
face
discussion.

✧ *Walter B. Pitkin*

desk. His boss regularly asks him to cover meetings in his stead, which means he has no time to complete his daily job tasks.

Compounding the situation, George's wife also has a position at a hospital and cannot always pick up the children in case of an emergency or illness. Their day care center is 10 miles from George's work and 15 miles from his wife's.

What are two steps George could take immediately to feel less stressed?

George needs considerable emotional support from both his wife and children. He must develop ground rules with his wife for open communications, or the relationship will deteriorate into a divorce. Part of that communication may include ways in which George and his wife can lead a simpler life so he would not be so pressured for his next promotion.

He should also reconsider the early morning exercise with his friend. This may be the prime time to spend time with his children. Possibly he could jog with the children in a running stroller, then have breakfast with his family.

They could find child care closer to their respective jobs. Also, making a specific date with his spouse each month might heal some old wounds. Sometimes time together alone is all that is needed.

Learning to say "no" without feeling guilty is essential for George's survival. He can, for example, acknowledge such requests, reply that he cannot do it, and then give viable alternatives: "I can see how important this project is for you. I must leave at 5 p.m. today, though we do have a couple of options. Let's see if anyone is still here who can help you with the project now. If not, I can rearrange my schedule for tomorrow and help you then. In the future, if you tell me before 2 p.m., I'll be able to help you right away."

Learning
is better
worth
than
house
or
land.

✦ *Crabbe*

Think about your own situation for a moment: Can you find an analogous solution for your own stress reduction? What might you do differently so you can turn stressful energy into a positive force?

Attitude management under stress

The experiences we accumulate and our perception of those experiences on a day-to-day basis become the filter through which our mindset develops. If your perceptions have been interpreted in a positive and forward-thinking manner, you will have an optimistic outlook. If the view has been one of despair and feeling out of control, you will have a pessimistic outlook.

Behavioral psychologists tell us that the first hour of each day is the most critical – and the most beneficial. Our minds are fresh, crisp and open to new ideas. The first hour of the day can make or break your success. Focus on the important and what you can control. What do you plan to do tomorrow? How will you greet the day?

Do you surround yourself with people who help you stay optimistic and in control? Al, my wonderful husband, has such a great outlook on life. He is rarely rattled by circumstances he cannot control and never upset by circumstances that he can't control when they do go awry. He has helped me focus on what is and what is not important in stressful events.

We often get muddled by the minutiae. I'm amazed at how simple life really is, and how complex we try to make it! But that gets back to choices and being positive. I choose to be positive and realistic. I really love it when people say, "Marsha is a little too perky for me." Working on optimism is a daily focus. I know that when I am positive, I attract positive people into my life. When I become toxic, I invite toxicity into my life. Remember, people like people who are more like them.

What
does not
destroy
me,
makes me
stronger.
* *Fredrick Wilhelm Nietzche*

The key: Every day is a new beginning. Treat it that way. Stay away from what might have been, and look at what can be.

The three stages of stress

If we understand the three stages of stress, we can keep ourselves from drifting into uncontrollable stress and sickness.

1. Alarm stage

Example: You discover the job you interviewed for has been held up because of budget constraints. Symptoms:

Fear	Depression
Disgust	Anger
Anxiety	Self-doubt

2. Resistance stage

You decide not to tell anyone how you feel and how disappointed you are. Symptoms:

Denial	Sensitivity
Aloneness	Irritability
Rejection	Exasperation

3. Exhaustion stage

Your situation does not change and you are still uncertain if you will ever get the new job. Symptoms:

Sleeplessness	Self-doubt
Erratic behavior	Illness, physical problems
Panic	Burnout

When you can identify where you are in your self-talk, you immediately reduce stress. Learning to accept and own your feelings will prevent the situation or event from overwhelming you. The importance of surrounding yourself with caring and supportive people is obvious. They will often give

There are
moments
when
everything
goes
well;
don't be
frightened,
it won't
last.
✧*Jules Renard*

a fresh and new perspective, but you must be willing to let them into your thoughts and feelings. When was the last time you really shared your inner feelings with a supportive loved one or friend?

Universal human needs

Understand that every human being has felt needs. Here are the nine common needs we all share. Rank them in order of importance (1 to 9) as you see them:

The need to feel important to yourself and in the eyes of others.

The need to be perceived as successful by yourself and others.

The need to be needed and wanted.

The need to feel useful.

The need to feel influential.

The need to be loved, appreciated, accepted and recognized by others.

The need to belong to something other than just yourself.

The need for adventure.

The need to experience growth in skills or learning.

When these needs are met, we remain stable and emotionally healthy. We are able to balance our lives and create energy and learning from stressful situations. I find it useful to look at this rank order once a year, and compare my rank order to last year's. What changed? Why? This in itself creates self-awareness and another tool to manage stress.

Why is this important? Flexibility! Learn from other people and create flexible options. The more situations you learn about, the more options you have.

When we realize we have choices, we feel more in control. When we are in control, we can be more flexible in our thinking and thus be more flexible in accepting change. Our lives and

We
struggle
with the
complexities
and
avoid
the
simplicities.
✦ *Norman Vincent Peale*

jobs become more dynamic. If we do not embrace change, we cannot stay motivated, and our performance suffers. Success eludes us.

I've come to realize that life has to be looked at one day at a time. We are not mind readers, and we never know from one day to the next what life will bring. We can plan, set goals, stay positive, and use every technique we've ever heard of, but flexibility is critical.

We sometimes feel that we have failed if we don't reach the goal exactly and by the deadline. Life is not an exact science and it does not come with an instruction book. New information is constantly washing over us. Daily events, especially the unexpected ones, can make us crazy.

So flexibility in thinking is really central in helping us to create additional options. I like Mark Twain's quip: "The only difference between a rut and a grave is the length and the depth." If you feel stressed out, maybe the small rut has become a self-fulfilling grave.

Why do so many stress themselves over situations or events they cannot change? Aging is one explanation. I'm not sure if I will grow old gracefully, but I do know I will do it with humor. Laughter releases endorphins that bring balance back into our lives. And please note: The natural endorphin hormone is much better and cheaper than Valium or Prozac.

Now for a little humor – the benefits of getting older:

The benefits of getting older

+ In a hostage situation, you are likely to be released first.
+ It's harder and harder for sexual harassment charges to stick.
+ Kidnappers are not very interested in you.
+ No one expects you to run into a burning building.
+ People call at 9 p.m. and ask, "Did I wake you?"
+ People no longer view you as a hypochondriac.
+ There's nothing left to learn the hard way.
+ Things you buy now won't wear out.
+ You buy a compass for the dashboard of your car.
+ You can eat dinner at 4 p.m.
+ You can live without sex but not without glasses.
+ You can't remember the last time you laid on the floor to watch television.
+ You consider coffee one of the most important things in life.
+ You constantly talk about the price of gasoline.
+ You enjoy hearing about other people's operations.
+ You lose your hearing aids and they're in your ears.

More benefits of getting older

+ You get into an intense argument about pension plans.
+ You got cable for the weather channel.
+ You have a party and the neighbors don't even realize it.
+ You no longer think of speed limits as a challenge.
+ You quit trying to hold your stomach in, no matter who walks into the room.
+ You send money to PBS.
+ You sing along with the elevator music.
+ You talk about "good grass" and you're referring to someone's lawn.
+ Your arms are almost too short to read the newspaper.
+ Your back goes out more than you do.
+ Your ears are hairier than your head.
+ Your eyes won't get much worse.
+ Your investment in health insurance is finally beginning to pay off.
+ Your joints are more accurate than the National Weather Service.
+ Your secrets are safe with your friends because they can't remember them either.
+ Your supply of brain cells is finally down to a manageable size.

Wisdom
consists
of the anticipation
of
consequences.

✦ *Norman Cousins*

Manage stress in the workplace

Stress occurs often in the workplace, whether you are an associate, employee, student, teacher, supervisor or chief. It doesn't matter if you are the receptionist (sometimes called "the rejectionist"), or the top dog; I can guarantee stress. So here are some suggestions and questions to ask yourself, whether you are a worker bee or the queen (or king) of the hive:

Strategies for worker bees

+ **Know the organization's mission, vision and goals.**
+ **Develop good work habits.**
+ **Learn good time management and prioritization skills and use them.**
+ **Stick by your to do list and compare it with your own and company goals.**
+ **Plan to procrastinate – because you will.**
+ **Eliminate what-if thinking – stick with your decision, but remember flexibility.**
+ **Learn to say "I made a mistake and here is what I learned."**

Strategies for the hive queen (or king)

+ **Let the worker bees determine the actions to achieve the objectives and goals.**
+ **Let them try it their way – they probably have a better way; if not, make sure instructions are clear.**
+ **Ask them for a reasonable deadline; if you don't agree, negotiate.**
+ **Deal with communication static by learning the four different styles of behavior and communication. Apply this in EVERY conversation.**
+ **Have daily or weekly meetings with your group – live or die by the time schedule of the meetings.**
+ **Grow your people – design specific, customized plans for each person, focusing on what they want to be when they grow up – not what you want them to be.**

As a well-spent day brings happy sleep, so a life well used brings happy death.

✧ *Leonardo da Vinci*

+ **Have and use a well-functioning employee assistance program, with the goal being sound mental health for all.**

Develop realistic expectations

Goal setting is the key to maintaining positive mental health. In this age of doing everything for everybody every time, maintaining good mental health is hard. Feeling in control and applauding improvements made in day-to-day life enhances emotional fitness. But nothing worthwhile is easy.

Here are five steps for maintaining mental fitness and health:

1. *Needs awareness* – Become more aware of your needs. If you don't like a particular segment of your life, recognize it and change it. Satisfaction with your job, relationships, and general environment is a must for sound development. If life gives you lemons, don't make just lemonade – bake a lemon meringue pie and lemon cookies, along with lemon cashew chicken! Work with what you have. Let others know what your needs are. People are not mind readers, and if you know they are supportive of you, communicate your needs and wants to them.

2. *Continually improve* – Be a lifelong learner, challenge yourself, get fit, and surround yourself with positive people. Enroll in a class, read a book, listen to a tape or watch an educational video. If you sharpen just one new (or old) skill, you have spent your time well. Challenge yourself to accept new ideas, hobbies, or anything that is different from what you currently do. Improve your fitness level through regular exercise, appropriate rest and good nutrition. Work on your spirit and soul by hanging around optimistic folks and then work on being perky – at least sometimes.

3. *Find your unique strengths* – Check your thinking when judging either yourself or others. Negative value judgments

Old
and
young,
we are
all
on our
last
cruise.
✦ *Robert Louis Stevenson*

consume too much energy. Focus on elements to admire and compliment, not only in others, but also in yourself. Look for the good qualities and give yourself and others credit. Record these strengths and accomplishments in a journal.

4. *Emergency escape route* – When you do have problems and failures, be prepared. Understand the self-talk before it happens, so you can stop that talk, recognize it, and change. This plan will help you when you set unrealistic high standards and are frustrated when they are not met. Don't wait for someone else to do this for you. Put on your own oxygen mask first, then assist others, as they say on the airplanes. You are no help to anyone, either at work or at home, if you are burned out.

5. *Volunteer* – When you give of yourself, you feed your soul. You can start by paying better attention to others and their needs during normal conversations. Focus your attention on the wants of others and identify what you can give them to be more successful.

Which of these five areas will you work on first? Write it down, set a deadline, and challenge yourself to enhance your mental fitness.

Stress management tools

Beware: Stress affects the physical self and can make you very ill and even lead to death. When you perceive stress from external or internal stimuli, a special stress message is sent to the hypothalamus, the pituitary gland, and the autonomic nervous system. Adrenaline flows. Blood pressure rises. Sugar floods the muscles, cholesterol and fats surge through the blood vessels, even blood clotting time is reduced.

If these physical stress events are never ending, your immune system is gradually damaged. Cholesterol counts

The
closer
to the
truth,
the
closer
to the
nerve.

✦*John M. Shanahan*

rise and serious health conditions result. Unmanaged stress is now recognized as a cause of premature aging, diabetes, some cancers, and even arthritis.

Tool 1 – Breathe

Example: You feel yourself moving to the alarm stage of stress (fear, depression, anger, anxiety). Place one hand flat on your stomach and breathe so your hand moves, not your shoulders. Make such breathing a conscious habit when you become aware of stress.

Watch someone who is under major stress. Their shoulders will heave and sag, because their breathing is shallow. All this does is exacerbate the stress, because little or no oxygen absorption occurs in the lower part of the lungs, clear thinking is inhibited. I recently noticed an infomercial that now sells an entire program on how to breathe. The target market is people who want to lose weight. Now there's a great side benefit of breathing properly!

Tool 2 – Mental exercises

Stress is a gift we give ourselves when we visualize all the negatives that may happen in a particular situation. Instead, picture the positive outcome. Talk to yourself about positive results. Remember, you become what you think about. Picture success. What is your mental picture and what are the positive mental exercises you have trained yourself to do?

Tool 3 – Physical exercise

Release endorphins by exercising. The hormone endorphin is an automatic stress reliever and brings a calming effect to your system. You only need to exercise 20 minutes a day and

If you can't stand the heat, get out of the kitchen.

⋄ *Harry Truman*

the minutes do not have to be consecutive. So think about parking a little bit further from the door. Take the stairs instead of the elevator. Pull your grocery bags out of the cart and carry them to the car. Walk to the mailbox instead of driving. Go for a bike ride or work in the yard. The more sedentary we are, the more stress will affect us.

Drink at least eight eight-ounce glasses of water per day to automatically flush toxins from your system. You are what you eat and drink.

Eat instant oatmeal in the morning instead of a donut. Have a baked potato with broccoli instead of a burger and fries. Order chicken or fish instead of red meat. I know, it's easier said than done.

Let yourself splurge every once in a while – just not at every meal! Carry raisins with you and chomp on them instead of candy. Have the celery and carrot sticks ready to snack on instead of the potato chips. Eat pretzels instead of corn chips. What's amazing about all of this is that you and I already know it – we just don't do it!

The next time you feel stressed, what will you do differently?

Typically, under stress, I would react opposite to the role models of my childhood. I had been exposed to yelling and anger, so I would become a clam – until I would hit the breaking point. Then the sarcasm, cynicism and closed mind would kick in. My first brain would close off to good ideas and solutions. This leads to ulcers and health problems. No longer will I allow lack of control to make me sick, stressed and out of control. Walking my talk is very important. I must say that, now in my 50s, I have never had more energy and felt more in balance in my life. I've learned to take stress and create energy from it.

The real
work
is putting
excitement
into your
work.

✦ *C.E. Jones*

Are you in balance? If not, why not? Are you willing to apply ideas that will put you more in control? To be less stressed? To grow old with grace?

The
most
difficult
thing
in life
is to
know
yourself.

❖ *Thales*

Chapter 6

✦

Unconscious competence

Emotional intelligence has become the new yardstick to measure the success of CEOs, junior hires, and anyone who wants to move to the next level in their job. In determining star performance in every field, emotional intelligence matters twice as much as cognitive abilities like IQ or technical expertise, according to research by Hay/McBer consultants.

The impact of emotional intelligence is even greater among top executives and leaders. If you want to be in a supervisory or management role, you start by developing emotional intelligence.

Emotional intelligence

So what is emotional intelligence? I agree with Dr. Daniel Goleman: Emotional intelligence is applying what we know to how we live. His work validated what CEOs and responsible people already know: Mastering your own emotions and understanding the emotions of the people around you is more than just being smart – it is the way you get things done! His work demonstrates how self-awareness, motivation, influence, conflict management, and team-building play out in today's business environment and the damage done when these qualities are absent.

The most important and admirable qualities you possess are the willingness to transform yourself through learning and self-discipline. Learning new ways to behave – with empathy, assertiveness, relationship building, innovation, and strategic thinking – increases emotional intelligence.

Go
to your
bosom,
knock
there,
and
ask
your heart
what it doth
know.

✦ *Shakespeare*

Bill Gates claims that 85 percent of our success is because of interpersonal skills and only 15 percent because of technical job skills. How important then is it to apply your interpersonal skills with consistency? During workshops, I try to send the message of using these skills not only at work, but also at home. The more you use a technique, the easier it becomes and the results continue to improve. Consistency becomes a habit, not an effort.

Such a habit of consistency forms the core of emotional intelligence – automatically being able to respond intelligently from the heart and the head, not just from reaction. This will also help us narrow the gap between how we know we should act and the way we really do. This gap can lead to guilt and stress if emotional intelligence is not used on a consistent basis.

Both the inner competencies that enable us to manage ourselves – ranging from self-awareness to motivation – and essential social strengths – such as influence, conflict management, and team-building – play out in some of the top corporations in the world today, including the damage done when they are lacking. When mergers, acquisitions and wholesale staff reductions take people out of their comfort zone, the consistent use of emotional intelligence becomes critical.

The hack 'em to pieces style of CEO "Chainsaw Al" Dunlap certainly stops the bleeding in a company heavy in debt and unprofitability. But I don't think many people want the moniker of "Chainsaw" – chopping heads off vs. understanding the issues at hand.

Our IQ is not necessarily the best measure of intelligence. I was a junior in high school when I was told not to bother with college because of my low IQ. The counselor's rationale was that the experts have found that students with a low IQ

Chaos often breeds
life, when
order breeds
habit.
✦ *Henry Brooks Adams*

will usually fail out in their first year. The recommendation for me? Take something of a vocational nature so I would be employable after high school. Having graduated with my MBA *magna cum laude*, shows that the traditional view of intelligence is too limited. I have friends and colleagues who claim to have very high IQs and they have not succeeded.

I agree with the experts' conclusion that understanding and managing emotions is at the core of success. So emotional intelligence really means:

- **Know yourself to manage yourself.**
- **Recognize others' emotions to manage others' emotions.**

Claiming the title of CEO for yourself is where you start. Obviously this validates the importance of developing emotional intelligence in childhood and strengthening and developing these skills throughout your life.

Whole brain change

We used to think that each person has a propensity to learn by either hearing information (auditory), seeing and reading information (visual), or working with information hands-on (kinesthetic). But here is a new term from the learning and training field: it's called "haptic."

We actually all learn in a haptic fashion – visually, auditorily and kinesthetically, all at the same time. Thus, when you understand how you learn, and embrace all three styles of learning, you can move forward to whole brain change.

Understand, too, that we are neither exclusively right- or left-brain thinkers. We blend both sides in the real world, sometimes lopsidedly. Have you ever heard someone say, "Well because I am left brained I am logical," or "because I am right

Cultivate
only
the
habits
that
you are
willing
should master
you.
✧ *Elbert Hubbard*

brained I get too emotional." We must learn to balance and use the whole brain. Being able to show emotion and empathy while thinking logically is the key to success. This is whole brain change and thinking.

You can find many learning-style inventory and assessment instruments that are statistically reliable and valid. I use these in my seminars, so leaders and workers understand how they usually operate. I am often surprised when people state that they have taken such an inventory, know where they are, but then don't apply what they have learned from the testing. When we know where we are coming from, and where other people are, we can be more flexible and begin using our whole brain. So why don't people use the information they know is useful?

I know I have a tendency to be very right brained, and seeing is believing most of the time for me. Understanding this, I can choose the areas to train myself in so that I operate from my whole brain. Hence, I've learned how to set goals using very specific steps and processes. Instead of shooting from the hip, I have trained myself to be a better communicator, with thoughtful responses rather than mindless reacting.

Do you use your whole brain? I am intrigued with people who say, "Well I've always been this way and I can never change." Simply put, this is a choice.

Whole brain thinking can help us in:

+ **Problem solving**
+ **Working in teams**
+ **Resolving conflict**
+ **Communicating at work**
+ **Communicating at home**
+ **Considering a career**

Our ability
to reach
unity
in
diversity
will be
the
beauty
and
test
of our
civilization.
✦ *Mahatma Gandhi*

At birth, the child's brain contains about 100 billion neurons. (These cells grow, eventually die, and are replaced, but the total number remains roughly the same.) Between each of these neuron cells is a cluster of connection pathways called a synapse. The first 15 years of life carve patterns into these synaptic connections. Because every experience is different and assessed differently, the synaptic patterns will be carved differently.

By a child's third birthday, the brain may be overwhelmed with information buzzing around inside. So for the next 10 years of development, the brain refines and focuses its growing network of connections.

The stronger synaptic connections – the ones that are reinforced more often – become stronger still. The weaker connections wither away. Dr. Harry Chugani, professor of neurology at Wayne State University Medical School, compares them to a highway system: "Roads with the most traffic get widened. The ones that are rarely used fall into disrepair." It's a kind of mental pruning.

Researchers have not defined why and how this happens. We do know that a child may develop a four-lane highway for empathy, feeling every emotion of those around them. If the empathy highway is in disrepair, the child may wind up with no understanding of empathy and be emotionally blind. Result? An inability to understand how others feel, and the child may say the wrong things at the wrong time, winding up frequently with foot-in-mouth syndrome. Obviously, the same holds true for confrontation, assertiveness, relationship building, innovation, strategic thinking and more.

The good news is that with enough training, encouragement, and coaching, you can repair and reopen the highway.

Till a man
can
judge
whether
they be
truths
or no, his
understanding
is but
little
improved,
and thus
men of much
reading,
though
greatly
learned,
but may
be little
knowing.

❖ *Locke*

You can change. After the teenage years, it is difficult to make that highway into a four-lane highway, but it is possible if the desire is there.

Our patterns make us and the people around us unique. The filter we all have is ours, and ours alone. It is like a fingerprint. It is yours, and yours alone. Do you like your filter? Do you like the fingerprint you leave?

Lifelong learning

Lifelong learning is sometimes hard. Often we don't apply what we already know, because the issue or the environment changes just enough to look like an entirely new problem. We experience a gap between what we know and what we think we know. But when we understand where we are in the process, we can see that gap. We can then understand what still needs to be learned, and therefore what skills/knowledge we still need to acquire. We then find it easier to take risks at learning, because we know the process.

Risks? Of course! Ask yourself, "What is the worst thing that can happen?" Then ask, "If that were to happen, what would be even worse?" And lastly, "What is the absolute worst outcome I could have."

A personal example: I am not a savvy techie – though I am willing to take a known risk when learning a new application on the computer. When I bought a scanner, I knew how to use PhotoShop – a little bit. But now I wanted to scan photos for my Web site and attach them to an e-mail to my Web master.

In the past, I would have talked myself out of even taking any risk and would have complained, "You don't know computers! All you will do is ruin everything!" So I picked up the scanner manual, read it (very unusual for me), and

Conquer
thyself. Till
thou
hast done
this, thou art
but a
slave;
for it is
almost
as well
to be
subjected
to another's
appetite
as to
thine
own.

⋄ *Burton*

successfully scanned a picture on my first try. I understood where I was, and I knew the desired outcome. This in itself helped me: By going from what I thought I knew to what I actually did know, I closed the gap.

The four levels of learning

Success at closing the gap comes more easily when you are clear about the four levels of learning:

Level 1 – The unconscious incompetent

You don't know what you don't know. This was my level when I started my first computer class in graduate school in 1981. I had no clue; I was petrified in front of a keyboard. I needed high direction and didn't care about the relationship with the person teaching me. I needed pure instruction.

Level 2 – The conscious incompetent

You are aware of what you don't know, you just can't do it very well. At this point, you need a coach who can give a high level of direction. The relationship becomes important. Constructive feedback is critical at this point, as are practice sessions.

Level 3 – The conscious competent

You are aware of what needs to be done and are able to do it, but you need much more practice to overcome mistakes. You need someone to lead in the right direction, like a facilitator, because you know you must have hands-on experience.

Level 4 – The unconscious competent

You are good! You do not have to think of the process because it has become rote. Tremendous ability has become the habit. You are unaware of how great you are because it is so simple. If anything, you may need a consultant when the

Learning
makes a man
fit
company
for
himself.

✧ *Young*

application or environment changes – just to run a few things past them.

As you learn new ideas, you move through these levels of learning. The problem with many professionals is that when they face a new task, they revert back to the unconscious incompetence or the conscious incompetence level. The ego often shows up. ("After all, I am a professional, and professionals do their job very well.")

Have you ever been in an environment where a decision was made to install and use an updated software program? You try to talk the decision maker into allowing you to keep using the old system, because it is so much easier for you. After all, it will take too much time to learn the new application. Then you realize that, with or without you, the new program is there, so you decide to read the documentation. Suddenly, you see the advantages to using the new software and you take on the new application with open arms. Soon you don't even remember the old software and can't imagine why others are having such a difficult time adapting! Here is the cycle:

You cannot
teach
a child
to take
care
of himself
unless you
will
let
him try
to take
care of
himself.
He will
make
mistakes;
and out of
these mistakes
will come
his
wisdom.

H.W. Beecher

When I worked at US West/Qwest, we saw this happen continually. People became complacent in their positions. The IBEW (International Brotherhood of Electrical Workers) and CWA (Communication Workers of America) represented many of our administrative and clerical support personnel. We were in the print advertising business, which had just begun to change at a very rapid pace. We now wanted to have our customer support people ask a few questions of our clients to determine new services, and potentially upgrade their advertising when appropriate. The union members were absolutely right when they said they didn't have to do it, because "it was not in the contract."

I believe that much of this reaction was caused by the need to take a new approach. Many of these people had been in the same position for more than 20 years. The process had hardly changed in those years. They had their comfort zone. These people were operating at the unconscious competence level.

This caused us to review our options for the business unit. We then discovered that selling the stable accounts to a competitor was our best choice: We could not compete. The personnel we had could have been terrific in moving our current clients to new levels of advertising and products. The problem we had was not just with the union members holding their ground, but our people not being able to change. If only we had known what we actually knew! Had these people understood how good they were and how life-long learning was an option, we would have been able to support the changes in our industry and for our clients. Some retired, some moved on to new positions outside the company, while others had a step-level change of grade and pay to position them where they actually fit

THE
CEO

HR

+ Selectively choose who is on your team

+ Select personal life services carefully

+ Hire the best people

PR

+ Establish a good first impression

+ At the end of every day, think of the five great events of the day

+ Get proper rest and exercise and start eating more healthily

+ Stay away from gossip

SALES

+ Develop an elevator speech

+ Sell YOU in 30 seconds or less

+ Stay caught up

+ Focus on what you have

CONTINGENCY PLANNING

+ Eliminate "what if" thinking

+ Visualize your next position

+ Encourage bootstrap thinking

+ Encourage flexibility

OF
YOU

R&D

+ Address the future

+ Invest 2 percent of your gross annual income in YOU

+ Do you know the goals of your company?

+ Be a lifelong learner

FINANCE

+ Lead a simpler life

+ Pay cash

+ Limit charge cards

+ Save money, even when you think you can't

IT

+ Hire a computer tutor

+ Embrace technology

within the restructured compensation and capability structure in the company.

With or without a union, this scenario continues to plague businesses today.

Innovation is hard work. Especially when we really know what we know, we must abandon our comfort zone, find the improvement needed and create the innovation. The critical need is to have the belief in ourselves that we can. Change is an opportunity. It cannot be seized without lifelong learning.

Revisit the diagram of the CEO across the page. Determine the learning needed for each of the departments of your life.

In the human resource department, have you built the relationships that maximize your success? Do you selectively choose each person you work with? If you have underperformers, are you helping them improve? Are you ready to replace any of them? What are you doing to maximize your investment in each person on your team? Learning program recommendation: *Gung Ho!* by Ken Blanchard and Sheldon Bowles.

Your sales department includes the marketing of YOU. Have you developed your elevator speech? When introducing yourself, have you learned to tell people what you do quickly and succinctly? Are you up-to-date on the market you perform in – reading and learning at every turn? Do you remind yourself on a frequent basis of your talents and seek out the next steps for improvement? Learning resource recommendation: *Confessions of Shameless Self Promoters* by Debbie Allen.

The research & development department prepares you for the unexpected, polishes tools you have, and provides new equipment and strategies for the future. Are you investing 2 percent of your gross annual income in YOU? Are you

The great
art
of
learning
is to
undertake
but little
at a
time.

✦ *Locke*

considerate and engaging in the goals of your company and the people around you? Learning resource recommendation: *Work Matters* by Tom Peters

Is contingency planning integral to your thinking? Does "what if" thinking energize you to see the possibilities, or become a barrier of future choices? Do you have a clear picture of your next steps and are you flexible if there is an unexpected issue? Is "flexible" your middle name – and do you continue to reaffirm life as an activity, not a spectator sport? Learning resource recommendation: *Go for the Gold* by your own Marsha Petrie Sue.

Public relations is basic for every CEO. Attitude, impression, communication, and all of the elements contained in perceptions are crowned in public relationships. Do you have resources available, both tangible and intangible, to change your outlook to optimism? Are you working daily to feel more healthy and centered? Do people clamor to have a conversation with you because you are engaging? Learning resource recommendation: *First, Break All the Rules* by Marcus Buckingham and Curt Coffman.

Your skill in the information technology field is critical. Practically using technology is no longer a nice-to-have tool, it is a must-have. Efficiency and effectiveness is the critical issue. Do you have a computer tutor? Do you read publications, resource guides and documentation to continually improve your skills? Are you on the lookout for advancements that help you be more productive? Learning resource recommendation: *Business At the Speed of Thought* by Bill Gates.

Finance is the cornerstone to being the CEO of YOU. You cannot succeed if you are constantly worrying where your next meal will come from or if the roof over your head is

We should
ask
not who
is the
most
learned but
who
is the best
learned.
✧ *Montaigne*

secure. Do you understand the financial instruments available and apply them appropriately to your financial goals? Are you aware of the level or risk you are willing to take? Do you fully understand exactly how much you will need on a day-to-day basis when you retire? Learning resource recommendation: *The Millionaire Next Door* by Thomas Stanley.

Challenge: What is your next step? What must you do starting right now? Making yourself available to opportunities is your job as CEO. The magic wand rests in your hand.

Men
must be
decided
on what
they
will
not
do,
and
then
they are
able
to set
with
vigor
in what
they
ought
to do.

⟡ *Mencius*

Chapter 7

✦

Solving the relationship puzzle

What makes relationships work? Flexibility and respect.

Flexibility is a learned skill which demands a willingness both to learn how to spot relationships that are headed for disaster and to develop elasticity in dealing with situations and people.

Inflexibility often creates a negative environment because there is no tolerance for another's point of view. It is destructive if overlooked or ignored.

Every human being deserves respect. We are each unique creations with a divine core of goodness. When we respect others, we set the tone for them to respect us. This does not mean they have to love us, just respect us. Don't expect everyone to become a best friend. The ability to respect their opinion and generally find out more about what they are thinking builds better connections.

Flexibility and respect help us build alliances that will last a lifetime.

How to break the cycle of negativity

You can break the cycle of negativity. Negative language begets negative reaction. Perceived pessimistic outcomes beget pessimistic reactions. Change the cycle of negativity by believing in miracles – you must first have the belief that the situation can change. Then you can open your mind to other solutions and opportunities to resolve differences. Try to stay

Defeat should never be a source of discouragement, but rather a fresh stimulus.

⬧ *Robert Southey*

focused on positive events. Read and listen to stories where positive outcomes prevail. When we change our thinking, miracles happen because we believe they can.

The cycle of negativity becomes worse if there is no relevance to the other person. Pessimistic approaches are often the result of not looking for another's point of view. Making the message relevant to the person you're addressing is the key to gaining their attention, especially in negative circumstances.

For example, let's look in on Fred, who is not known to be a positive contributor in his workplace. He is good at his job and loves the data and statistics of projects, but a hostile audience awaits Fred at his upcoming presentation. He needs their buy-in. His PowerPoint show is ready to roll and he is well practiced. But the little voices in his head keep telling him he is going to fail. Tough information + hostile audience = negative outcome. The cycle of negativity has begun. Another self-fulfilling prophecy?

By his second slide, someone yells, "So what's the point? You are giving us too much detail!" Flustered, Fred continues until another voice interrupts him again, "What's the bottom line here? You are not addressing the opportunity, only the problem."

Fred retaliates with, "Well this is the problem and if you don't have the detail, you will never understand the solution." He plods from slide to slide. Muttered comments continue to fill the room. Fred finishes, the group says nothing and leaves.

The group is frustrated. Fred is upset. His self-talk goes: "See, I knew it. I just knew it would end this way! We'll never finish this project because they just don't get it!" The cycle of negativity goes on and on and on. What each of us needs at such times are some techniques to break the cycle of negativity.

Children
have
more
need
of
models
than of
critics.

⋄ Joubert

Change your communication choices

Breaking the cycle of negativity can be viewed from different angles. Sometimes the most intelligent way to deal with negativity is to make sure your message does not reinforce an existing attitude. Choose neutral language.

Road signs exemplify this. Notice that nowadays you rarely see highway signs that say, "Slower traffic keep right." Such word choice upsets many, because it means if you are in that lane you may be incompetent, unqualified, or just plain incapable of driving in the faster lane. Notice how more modern signs now read, "Use left lane for passing only." The stigma is gone; the message has been neutralized.

When you have the opportunity to resolve a situation with another person or group, consider using nonthreatening language like this:

"I would like to better understand when you . . ."

"Help me understand . . ."

"Where are you coming from when you say . . ."

"Can we schedule some time to talk about . . ."

Choose your words carefully. When you use absolutes (such as "must," "never," "under no circumstances") you will usually raise hackles in tenuous conversations. Intensifiers (such as "most," "latest," "least") can also raise the level of anger during communications.

When you want relationships to work, pay attention to your words. Listening to what you say and caring about the perception of the other person become important. Shooting from the hip is no longer an option and every conversation counts.

We know that once the words are spoken, they can never be taken back. The message is there, no matter how hard we

The
soul
without
imagination
is what
an
observatory
would be
without
a
telescope.
❖ *H.W. Beecher*

try to erase it. Retaliatory remarks like "Oh, just forget about it!" are useless, because once said, they can never be retracted.

When you extend yourself to others, whether at work or at home, it feels good. The problem is when this action is not recognized and reinforced by others, we may withdraw and stop giving. We wait to receive before giving again. Don't let others dictate how generous you are or will be.

Have you tried this technique? Write a letter (that will not be sent) to the person who has not acknowledged your generosity. Fill in the blanks:

> *Dear* _____
> *I am irritated/upset that* _____
> *I am frustrated/sad that* _____
> *I am afraid that* _____
> *I am embarrassed and am sorry that* _____
> *I understand/forgive/trust you for* _____
> *I love you.*
> *Sincerely, your name*

Don't send this! If need be, write out an apology you would like to hear from the person in a non-demanding manner. When your good deed is not recognized, it's OK. Move on. Don't feed the cycle of negativity – break it!

Do your homework

Let's revisit a more flexible Fred and his PowerPoint presentation. Let's see if respect comes to him as he breaks the cycle of negativity.

At his second slide, someone yells, "So what's the point? You are giving us too much detail!" Flustered, Fred continues,

The
closer
one gets
to the
top,
the more
one
finds
there is no 'top.'

✦ *Nancy Barcus*

but another voice interrupts him again asking, "What's the bottom line here? You are not addressing the opportunity, only the problem!" Overcoming his anxiety, Fred flips to the last slide, a total recap and graph of the problem and the solution. He confidently walks his audience through the process. Someone claps wildly: "Now that's what we wanted to hear! Can you present this again tomorrow to the big guns?" Thrilled but baffled, Fred agrees.

What happened here? Although Fred was more flexible, he did not get close enough to his listeners beforehand to know about their expectations, their frame of reference, and what might be relevant to their needs. He needed to prepare, which takes more time up front, but saves time in the long run.

The best practice is to do your homework, whether one-on-one or one-on-many. Fred was able to walk away from the meeting, knowing he had been flexible, even if he didn't completely prepare for his audience adequately. Because he was flexible, the outcome could be positive. He broke the cycle of negativity.

Choose your battles

Few decisions are worth making a fuss over. Ask yourself, "Do I really care?" This will keep fights from spinning out of control. Two key points are needed to keep fights from getting really ugly:

1) *De-escalate the argument before it gets out of control.* Here's a great ground rule: Prior to any argument, enable either party to call a time-out or a ceasefire before either party (or both) fly out of control. Another way is to bring up a positive. People stop listening when they feel criticized. Good language: "I know your intentions are good. I don't want you

To
think
is easy.
To
act
is hard.
But
the
hardest
thing
in the
world
is to
act
in accordance
with your
thinking.

✦ *Johann Goethe*

to think I am minimizing this in any fashion." And listen for areas of agreement.

2) Talk about the conflict in an open, honest way. If there is too much furor at the time, set a date to revisit the issue. Don't bring up difficult subjects when anger permeates the conversation. Good language: "I'm upset. This is not a good time for me to continue, and I'd like to wait until I'm not so mad."

Commit yourself both personally and professionally to praise the traits you appreciate or admire. The more often you do this, the more responsive the other person will become. Develop solid consistency in such behavior, because when you must discuss a negative, the other person has not been inundated with negatives and problems.

Save criticism for what is really important. If you don't, you are not choosing your battles. Constant criticism and inappropriate criticism (being picky) erode the alliances you work so hard to build.

When someone's actions affect the needed outcome, begin by telling the person something they do well or have done well. Then share the improvement needed that will result in a more appropriate outcome.

Another example: Joan has been assigned a project and missed the deadline. What's even worse is that her objective was way off target.

Instead of approaching Joan with "You should have," or "You could have," change your approach to: "Joan, that format you used was terrific. I would have never thought of it. Next time we need to make sure the objective and the deadline are met, because we missed both this time. Let's take two steps for more positive results: Because I know some of these projects are really complex, I will put the expected objectives and the

Winner vs. Loser

The winner – is always part of the answer
The loser – is always part of the problem

The winner – always has a program
The loser – always has an excuse

The winner – says, "Let me do it for you"
The loser – says, "That's not my job"

The winner – sees an answer for every problem
The loser – sees a problem for every answer

The winner – sees a green near every sand trap
The loser – sees two or three sand traps near every green

The winner – says, "It may be difficult but it's possible"
The loser – says, "It may be possible but it's too difficult"

Be a winner!

deadline in writing. Then I will hear them back from you in your own words. That way we can both be sure we're clear about the project. Is that something we, as two professionals, can agree on?"

You thus defuse the conflict. Joan will almost certainly choose not to go to battle on this subject. You have helped her to focus instead on the needed outcome.

Explain why you feel the way you do. People are not mind readers. We may think they should know and may communicate, even nonverbally, the message, "Well, if you don't know, I'm not going to tell you!" Full battle armor goes on and the war has begun.

I've said such things many times in my younger days. I now realize how immature that was. When you explain yourself, you keep from being polarized and stuck. Once the scud missile is launched, then we are at war.

Finding a third alternative may resolve a thorny issue. Create a win-win; good for them and good for me. Compromise, on the other hand, is not always positive, because often someone feels they have given up too much. Win-win means I feel as good about the resolution as you do.

If you choose not to grapple with these issues, the negative cycle continues, pulling people, relationships, and teams down, down, and down. The results? Stress, poor communications and ultimately, poor relationships.

Copy the poem opposite and hang it up in your office.

Defuse arguments with family members

You have probably already learned that trying to reason with a family member does not always work and may prolong the argument and even raise the level of tension. Some simple and seemingly counterproductive techniques can work.

What we do upon some great occasion will probably depend on what we already are: and what we are will be the result of previous years of self-discipline.

H.P. Liddon

End debates quickly. You do this by firmly stating your position, possibly repeating it, and then move on. Reason? To let the other person know you've made up your mind and no amount of begging or whining will change your mind.

For example, let's say a member of your family is notorious for leaving his belongings strewn throughout the house. You ask him to pick up after himself; you are accused of being unfair. He responds with an impatient, "That's not all my stuff. Some belongs to you. Why do I have to clean up after you? You never clean up after me!"

Try to stay away from a response that is defensive, such as, "Everyone in this house pitches in. Mary helps when she is asked, so you should, too." Or worse, "Who do you think I am – the maid?" Such defensive responses will typically escalate to higher levels of emotion.

A better response may be, "I need your help. I will be able to spend more time with you if you put away your things." The difficulty here is not to raise the tone of your voice, which does nothing but engage the other person in a fight.

Your young people are probably better behaved in the outside world than they are with you. The good news is that this is usually because they are comfortable with you!

One way to build a better relationship is to create ground rules to maintain consistency in behavior. This is especially true with children and they learn quickly. The famous game of "if one doesn't say 'yes,' maybe the other one will," still exists and, in the child's mind, allows bartering and negotiating with adults. Consistency is the name of the game, and ground rules establish this consistent boundary with your children, or even your partner.

Here is a great reminder –

If I had my child to raise all over again,
I'd build self-esteem first and the house later.
I'd finger paint more and I'd point the finger less.
I would do less correcting, and more connecting.
I'd take my eyes off my watch, and watch with my eyes.
I would care to know less, and know to care more,
I'd take more hikes, and fly more kites.
I'd stop playing serious, and seriously play.
I would run through more fields, and gaze at more stars.
I'd do more hugging and less tugging.
I'd see the oak tree in the acorn more often.
I would be firm less often, and affirm much more.
I'd model less about the love of power
and more about the power of love.

Faxed to me from Rhonda Finness - Canada

Fixing team relationships

Diversity is the defining characteristic of the best teams. You've seen them all: the strugglers and the sprinters; the logical and the eccentric; the controllers and the strugglers; the Pollyannas, relaters and socializers – all typically contribute to a team's success. If there is any dissension or problem between the members, the entire team process can come to a screaming halt. Poor relationships become barriers to success.

Team members usually need help in de-escalating issues. Being a mind reader helps – it's always nice to see what can happen as a situation unfolds without your intervention. Seriously though, simply being aware of irritations can better position you for the next encounter of the fiercer kind.

To keep a team running smoothly, set up some specific guidelines. For example, how does the team want to communicate and what are the behaviors expected of each member?

Here are five more thoughts on the cycle of negativity in teams:

- *Disapproval and criticism* – People are afraid they will not fit in with the rest of the group. Or if they do try to change and improve, they fear they will be criticized by their peers. It is not easy to face the disapproval and criticism of others.
- *Fear of humiliation and ridicule* – Strugglers are afraid that if they try something new, their peer group may humiliate them. For example, a new person is brought into the group. Initially, the members like and want to welcome this new person. But a co-worker sees them reaching out to this person and ridicules them into shunning the newbie. Too bad. Have you ever gone against the flow of the group, only to find yourself retreating?

The virtue of a man ought to be measured not by his extraordinary exertions, but by his everyday conduct.

✦ *Blaise Pascal*

- *Fear of decision making* – Status quo is good for the strugglers. They don't want to overextend themselves or stand up for something they know needs to be done.
- *Jealousy and envy* – Both are dangerous. Becoming aware of the language we choose will help us move away from struggling with others' successes. If you hear your self-talk – "I am jealous of their success," "I envy her position" – why not set a new success goal for yourself? When you become resentful or begin to suspect others' motives, you harm yourself in the extreme. Jealousy means distrust and mistrust. Envy on the other hand is true hatred or dislike. Both emotions force struggling to even deeper levels. They can drown our success.
- *Fear of failure* – When people have failed in the past, they don't ever want to have that feeling again. So they stop taking risks. "What will Joan think if this doesn't turn out well?" "Will Harry think ill of me if I succeed?" Always ask yourself, what is the worst thing that can happen? Then be truthful with yourself! Motivate the struggler to go from being a victim to being a victor. Here's a new motto for strugglers: *Starve problems, find opportunities.*

Determine potential problem areas

The adage, "One bad apple spoils the whole barrel," does not have to happen to your team. The one bad apple is often a struggler. I define this person as someone who continues to proceed with great difficulty or with great effort because of their inability to take responsibility for their actions. Just be aware of what to look for in struggler behaviors and how they influence the team. If the struggler is a "bad apple," then the whole team's work is in jeopardy.

You can't
talk
your way
out
of problems
you
behave
yourself
into.
✦ *Stephen R. Covey*

Here are six indicators that your struggler is affecting team outcomes:

+ He has poor speaking skills when communicating with the team: she doesn't make her points clear; he becomes a clam and says nothing; she rambles, mumbles and often speaks too softly; he doesn't make eye contact.
+ She is incongruent: What she says and what she actually does are far apart; other team members sense that there is more going on than meets the eye.
+ He talks a lot: He fills air space, but says nothing and no one responds.
+ She becomes arrogant and even bullying: She may say things like, "What you don't understand is..."
+ He uses softeners that dilute and diffuse his message. He becomes plaintive – "This may sound dumb but...", "I may be wrong, but...", or the classic personal put-down favorite, "Can I ask a question?"
+ She discounts others' opinions, like "That's not important. What's worse is..."

Stopping this process before it even is noticed by the majority is the real key. Be on the lookout, because otherwise the cycle of negativity continues.

Breaking the cycle of team negativity

Help the strugglers develop communication skills and recognize problems that result from poor communication:

+ Take time to create a meeting evaluation session to talk about how well team members communicate.
+ Set ground rules with the team members on how they should communicate during meetings.
+ Have outside observers (I call this the fish bowl technique) give the group honest feedback on its communication dynamics. Or better yet, videotape the meeting and review what you see and hear. Take this a step further and watch the videotape with the sound off. Our communication is approximately 55 percent of what people actually see. Do you like what you see and hear?

No one
is
useless
in this
world
who
lightens
the burdens
of
another.

❖ *Charles Dickens*

Team guidelines

Beneficial team behaviors need to become known and accepted as ground rules. Before the first meeting, decide how the team members will communicate, and what behavior is expected of each team member. If you help the team members develop such specific rules, they will feel ownership of them and will buy into the team's efforts. Eleven considerations:

+ **Initiate discussions.**
+ **Have one conversation at a time.**
+ **It's OK to disagree and disagreement does not equal dislike.**
+ **Seek information and opinions.**
+ **Suggest procedures for reaching a goal.**
+ **Summarize and determine action items, a timeline and who is responsible.**
+ **Begin and end meetings on time.**
+ **Have a gatekeeper and a timekeeper to stick to the agenda.**
+ **Compromise and be creative in resolving differences.**
+ **There are no dumb questions.**
+ **Test for consensus.**

Build a STAR team

I have worked on many teams and have been involved in training team management. Any team can be a STAR team – one that focuses on four dynamic areas: Skill, Treaty, Agreement, and Recognition.

Skill – Recognize and maximize the skills of each member. Not everyone needs to know how to do everything, but everyone knows how to do something. That is the true strength of a team – which means each member must use their learned skills with confidence. They must be able to reach into their toolbox and use some of the gear they've not used for a while.

The ultimate measure of a man is not where he stands in moments of comfort and convenience, but where he stands at times of challenge and controversy.

✦ *Martin Luther King, Jr.*

Treaty – Selflessness instead of self. Members must have shared objectives and a sense of values. Team success depends on members keeping their eyes on the goal – sometimes a member must put the team first. When that happens, they must see that their needs get met quicker and more effectively.

Agreement – Teams must agree on the process and the plan. We see many sport teams that have fantastic, highly paid athletes who by themselves have been very successful. Then when thrust into a team environment, it's all about them, not the team. Michael Jordan was exactly the opposite. His extraordinary ability enhanced his team, but his willingness to help others succeed brought the Chicago Bulls six world championships.

Recognition – Ken Blanchard says, "Behavior that is recognized will be repeated." I'll take that a step further and say, "Behavior that is recognized AND REWARDED will be repeated." Why do coaches stand on the sidelines and scream at the players? Tear them down after a loss? Why do some leaders only tell their workers everything they do wrong? And remind them on their appraisals?

The better model is John Wooden, the UCLA men's basketball coach, whose winning record is a success story in itself. He didn't yell or scream. He supported success and rewarded change.

Let's face it: You cannot change the past. You can only change the future.

Your challenge: To improve relationships you must understand how you are perceived by others. Ask for feedback, listen to recordings of your voice, hear the words you are using and watch for the effects of your communications. Ask yourself: "If I could improve just one element of me, what would that be?"

Your team is ready to be a STAR!

Winners are everyday heroes.

Winners take their dreams seriously.

Winners never give up and won't let you give up, either.

Winners have attitude.

Winners care in their sleep.

Winners make big things happen a little at a time.

Winners say "Yes" to freedom and change.

Winners go with the flow.

Winners see the beginning in every ending.

Winners expect the best.

Winners inspire the best in others.

Winners are the richest people in the world when it comes to experience, laughter, and love.

Winners have chosen to be the CEO of themselves!

Evaluate your striving talents of desire, competence, belief, ethics, and stamina. Understand your thinking talents of focus, discipline, and responsibility. Appraise your relating talents of empathy, perception, enthusiasm, optimism, and courage. Include how you are measuring your performance and success, problem-solving techniques, strategic thinking, and creativity.

What one idea has been refreshed, renewed or learned that will move you to the next level?

What one element will allow you to be a better CEO of YOU?

Love is never lost. If not reciprocated it will flow back and soften and purify the heart.

✦*Washington Irving*

Take Marsha Home!

Don't miss these resources.
For more information visit www.MarshaPetrieSue.com.
BLOG: www.DecontaminateToxicPeople.com

Toxic People: decontaminate difficult people at work without using weapons or duct tape (Book)

#1 Best Seller on Barnes and Noble and CEO Read

There are some horrible people at work: Steamrollers, Zipper Lips, Know-It-Alls, Back Stabbers, Needy Weenies, Whine and Cheesers -- the list goes on.

You don't have to let them suck the life out of you and your team. Marsha Petrie Sue provides the symptoms and relief for Toxic People and difficult behavior. She will help you identify your own toxicity, explain how to cure toxic infections, and become a better person, in case you suddenly recognize the toxic signs in yourself!

Toxic People: Quick and Easy Mobile Mentor (2 CD set)

Learn how to manage difficult people on the run. This two CD set is the perfect accompaniment to the book outlining the essence of the Barnes and Noble best seller, *Toxic People.*

Visit www.MarshaPetrieSue.com and sign up for Marsha's ezine (online newsletter) and receive a great gift.

Ignite your next meeting by bringing in Marsha. She is known as the Muhammad Ali of communications. Marsha can dance and look pretty, and she uses the entire ring, but she knows how and when to land a knockout punch. Get the smelling salts! Her presentations are charm school with live ammunition.

1.866.661.8756 or 480.661.8756 info@MarshaPetrieSue.com

Who is Marsha Petrie Sue?

Marsha is an award-winning author and international speaker leading workshops and presenting keynotes throughout the United States, Africa, Europe and the Pacific Rim.

Her groups include public, private and government institutions, businesses, associations and corporations.

The participants of her presentations praise her energy, humor, charisma, professional delivery and depth of knowledge. She leaves the audience with practical advice and methods for success.

As a leadership and professional development expert, Marsha works with companies that want to improve profitability and productivity. An extensive background in executive leadership and management with Fortune 500 companies gives her the depth and breadth of knowledge and wisdom to provide valued information.

Topics include:
- Ethics and integrity
- Emotional intelligence
- Managing change
- Presentation skills
- Communication and conflict management

Personal Mission: To give back more than she has received and connect her head and heart with her mouth.

Living in Scottsdale, Arizona, Marsha and her husband Al enjoy the outdoors, golf and gardening. She really did marry a boy named Sue!

You may contact Marsha Petrie Sue, MBA, these ways:
Voice: 480-661-8756   Fax: 480-661-8755
PO Box 15218, Scottsdale, AZ 85267
Email: Marsha@CommunicatingResults.com
www.communicatingresults.com